THE LITTLE BOOK OF

Race and Restorative Justice

Published titles include:

The Little Book of Restorative Justice: Revised & Updated,
by Howard Zehr
The Little Book of Conflict Transformation, by John Paul Lederach
The Little Book of Family Group Conferences, New Zealand Style,
by Allan MacRae and Howard Zehr
The Little Book of Strategic Peacebuilding, by Lisa Schirch
The Little Book of Strategic Negotiation, by Jayne Seminare Docherty
The Little Book of Circle Processes, by Kay Pranis
The Little Book of Contemplative Photography, by Howard Zehr
The Little Book of Restorative Discipline for Schools,
by Lorraine Stutzman Amstutz and Judy H. Mullet
The Little Book of Trauma Healing, by Carolyn Yoder
The Little Book of Biblical Justice, by Chris Marshall
The Little Book of Restorative Justice for People in Prison,
by Barb Toews
The Little Book of Cool Tools for Hot Topics,
by Ron Kraybill and Evelyn Wright
El Pequeño Libro de Justicia Restaurativa, by Howard Zehr
The Little Book of Dialogue for Difficult Subjects,
by Lisa Schirch and David Campt
The Little Book of Victim Offender Conferencing,
by Lorraine Stutzman Amstutz
The Little Book of Restorative Justice for Colleges and Universities,
by David R. Karp
The Little Book of Restorative Justice for Sexual Abuse,
by Judah Oudshoorn with Michelle Jackett and Lorraine Stutzman Amstutz
The Big Book of Restorative Justice: Four Classic Justice &
Peacebuilding Books in One Volume,
by Howard Zehr, Lorraine Stutzman Amstutz, Allan MacRae, and Kay Pranis
The Little Book of Transformative Community Conferencing,
by David Anderson Hooker
The Little Book of Restorative Justice in Education,
by Katherine Evans and Dorothy Vaandering
The Little Book of Restorative Justice for Older Adults,
by Julie Friesen and Wendy Meek
The Little Book of Racial Healing,
by Thomas Norman DeWolf and Jodie Geddes

The Little Books of Justice & Peacebuilding present, in highly accessible form, key concepts and practices from the fields of restorative justice, conflict transformation, and peacebuilding. Written by leaders in these fields, they are designed for practitioners, students, and anyone interested in justice, peace, and conflict resolution.

The Little Books of Justice & Peacebuilding series is a cooperative effort between the Center for Justice and Peacebuilding of Eastern Mennonite University and publisher Good Books.

THE LITTLE BOOK OF

Race and Restorative Justice

Black Lives, Healing, and US Social Transformation

FANIA E. DAVIS

New York, New York

Good Books books may be purchased in bulk at special discounts for sales promotion, corporate gifts, fund-raising, or educational purposes. Special editions can also be created to specifications. For details, contact the Special Sales Department, Good Books, 307 West 36th Street, 11th Floor, New York, NY 10018 or info@skyhorsepublishing.com.

Good Books is an imprint of Skyhorse Publishing, Inc.®, a Delaware corporation.

Visit our website at www.goodbooks.com

10 9 8 7 6 5 4 3 2 1

Library of Congress Cataloging-in-Publication Data

Names: Davis, Fania, author.
Title: The little book of race and restorative justice: black lives, healing, and US social transformation / Fania Davis.
Description: New York NY: Good Books, 2019. | Series: Little books of justice and peacebuilding
Identifiers: LCCN 2018057655 (print) | LCCN 2018060299 (ebook) | ISBN 9781680993448 (eBook) | ISBN 9781680993431 (paperback)
Subjects: LCSH: Restorative justice—United States. | African Americans—Social conditions—1975- | African Americans—Legal status, laws, etc. | BISAC: LAW / General. | SOCIAL SCIENCE / Minority Studies. | LAW / Civil Rights.
Classification: LCC HV8688 (ebook) | LCC HV8688 .D38 2019 (print) | DDC 305.896/073—dc23
LC record available at https://lccn.loc.gov/2018057655

Series editor: Barbara Toews
Cover photograph: Howard Zehr

Paperback ISBN: 978-1-68099-343-1
eBook ISBN: 978-1-68099-344-8

Printed in Canada

Table of Contents

1.
The Journey to Racial Justice and Restorative Justice

AKOBEN

Akoben is a traditional wind instrument used to summon warriors to the battlefield. May we be alert, devoted, and prepared to serve a good cause.

The field of restorative justice arose in the mid-1970s in the United States out of disaffection with the dysfunction of our prevailing justice system, in an effort to transform the way we think about and do justice. This was a new but old justice dawning on the stage of human history. During its first forty years, however, the restorative justice (RJ) community largely failed to address race, quite surprisingly given that it is people of color who overwhelmingly bear the brunt of the horrific inequities of our nation's criminal justice system, past and present. Just as the restorative justice community has historically failed to adopt a racial or social justice stance, few racial justice activists embrace restorative justice. Calling for a convergence of the two, this *Little Book of Race and Restorative Justice* urges racial justice advocates to invite more healing energies into their lives and restorative justice advocates to bring more warrior energies into theirs.

My intent in invoking healer and warrior archetypes warrants clarification. I do not use "warrior" in its oppositional or militaristic sense, but in its spiritual valence, connoting the integration of power and compassion, as embodied in the bodhisattva, or warrior-sage. The fierce African Maasai warriors, whose foremost concern is with the well-being of the children, also come to mind. In an example closer to home, I think of the indigenous youth activists at Standing Rock who led the historic resistance to the Dakota Access Pipeline installation in 2016 and who engaged in ceremony as a form of social action, proclaiming they were water and earth protectors, not simply protestors.

Nor do I use the term "healer" to connote one who works to heal the human body. Rather, I use it more broadly to mean one who aspires to heal the *social* body, or transform social harm. Our nation was born in the horrific traumas of genocide and slavery. Because we have neither fully acknowledged nor reckoned with these twin traumas, much less worked to heal them, they perpetually reenact themselves transgenerationally. We who dedicate our lives to social change have a chance to succeed only if we also devote ourselves to individual and collective healing.

Restorative justice and the indigenous ethos in which it is grounded (fully discussed in Chapter 2) are strongly relational in their orientation. Both deeply value entering into and maintaining "right relationship" as well as sharing one's personal story. Indigenous protocol invites us to introduce ourselves through ancestors, lineage, and land. And so I open this book by introducing myself and recounting how I came to embrace both racial justice and restorative justice, following the way of the warrior and healer.

Born during the segregation era in Birmingham, Alabama, post-genocidal land of the Creek, Cherokee, Chickasaw, Choctaw, and Alabama people, I am a descendant of West African captives forcibly removed during the transatlantic slave trade to North America. My and my three siblings' mother, Sallye B. Davis, and father, B. Frank Davis, migrated from Alabama's countryside to the industrial hub of Birmingham during the 1930s.

Our mother, a woman of courage and vision, ran away from home to Birmingham when only fourteen years old to follow her dream of enrolling in the only black high school in the state. At that tender age, she defied her foster parents, who insisted that, after graduating from elementary school, she begin domestic work for white people, as was then the custom. Our mother went on to complete high school and become one of the first blacks in Alabama to earn a graduate degree in early childhood education. Our father, the first in his family to graduate from college, was also the first black to own an automotive business and parking lot in downtown Birmingham, located in what is now known as the Civil Rights District.

Founded in 1871, Birmingham was the southern center of mining, railroading, and iron and steel production, designed to exploit the cheap, nonunionized labor of newly freed Africans, giving it a competitive edge over northern cities. By the 1960s, when my siblings and I were growing up, it was the most racially segregated city in the nation, dubbed "Bombingham" because of the frequent bombings intended to terrorize churches and individuals active in the civil rights movement.

We lived on "Dynamite Hill," a neighborhood regularly bombed because it was home to black families who dared move into the previously all-white neighborhood, formerly an antebellum slave plantation. We were fortunate our home was never struck, but the nightmarish explosions of bombs targeting our neighbors' homes jarred us awake during the early hours of the morning. Fathers in the neighborhood organized an armed patrol in self-defense; and, at times, our father, awakened by the noise of footsteps, would grab his gun and run outside to reconnoiter, fearful that terrorists lurked nearby.

Everything was segregated—schools, churches, parks, libraries, movies, and neighborhoods. This segregation extended to relationships. Police detained my father and a white out-of-town visitor simply because they were riding in a car together. My older sister participated in an interracial discussion group at First Congregational Church, our home church, and for that reason was targeted for bombings. Racial terror was part of our daily life. I later came to understand these conditions were virtually indistinguishable from South African apartheid.

As a child, I was surrounded by black people fighting for change. Arthur D. Shores, a legendary civil rights attorney, lived just across the street from our church. My sister and I were friends with his daughters. Attorney Shores litigated landmark cases before the US Supreme Court: cases vindicating voting rights; ending segregation in housing, public schools, and the state university; stopping police terror and racial discrimination in unions; and securing equal pay for Birmingham's black schoolteachers. He also represented Dr. Martin Luther King Jr. and thousands of others during Birmingham's civil rights protests of the 1960s. His work made him a target, and his home was bombed three times; he took to sitting on the porch at night, armed with a shotgun. At a young age, I was transfixed by and felt a kinship with Lawyer Shores. While short in stature, he was a colossus and warrior for justice in my eyes.

Our mother was also a longtime social justice activist. In the 1930s, she served as an officer in the Southern Negro Youth Congress, a progressive anti-racist organization, and helped lead the work of the Unemployed Councils. These councils formed during the 1930s to protest mass unemployment and inadequate relief and worked to free the Scottsboro Brothers, nine young black men (ages thirteen to twenty) falsely accused of raping two white women. Her activism continued into the 1940s in the anti-fascist movement, the 1950s and '60s in the civil rights movement, and later, in the 1970s in the international campaign to free her daughter (my sister) Angela Davis, who was a political prisoner at the time. During the early 1980s, my mother served as consultant to the Ministry of Education in socialist Grenada before the US invasion. While we were growing up, our mother's voice was a powerful antidote to pervasive social messaging that declared black people subhuman, ever instilling a deep confidence that we should never feel ourselves inferior to whites.

As a preteen, I developed a visceral response to injustice and engaged in my own spontaneous acts of resistance—for instance, deliberately sitting in the "whites only" section in the front of the bus, drinking water from white fountains, and entering white restrooms. I always managed to escape arrest, even when police were called. Some acts of resistance were humorous. My sister and I were learning French, and while we were downtown one day, we pretended to be French-speaking foreigners. With heavy French accents, we inquired about shoes in an upscale store. Spellbound by the exotic, the store clerks seated us in the front of the store, not the back as was protocol for black customers. They rolled out the red carpet. After a few minutes of trying on shoes and communicating with strained English and gestures, my sister and I burst out laughing. The sales clerks laughed along politely, asking what was so funny. In our black southern English, we responded: "All black people have to do is pretend to come from another country, and you treat us like dignitaries." We triumphantly sashayed out of the store.

Our mother resolved to send all her children to well-resourced high schools in the North as an alternative to finishing high school in the separate, unequal, and under-resourced schools of the South. I subsequently left in 1962, at fifteen years old, to attend a New Jersey high school under the auspices of the Quakers' Southern Negro Student Project. This project extended cultural and educational opportunities to black students from the Jim Crow South by placing them with white families in northern cities so they could attend nonsegregated high schools during their junior and senior years. I lived with a Polish family who escaped fascism's concentration camps and fled to the United States in the 1940s. I was thrilled to be part of this brand-new and exciting world. My host family exposed me to New York's museums and bohemian art scene. This was a whole new world—I was living and socializing with white people and exploring their culture for the first time.

It did not take long, however, to discover that racial discrimination existed up North too, though it was expressed more subtly. My classmates invited my host sister, who was my age, to social events but snubbed me. Teachers made offensive comments about my hair, while students made fun of my southern drawl. The only black student in my class, I was socially isolated. I responded by devouring James Baldwin's *The Fire Next Time* and other racial justice texts of the times. I militantly spoke out in class on current racial justice issues. I attended demonstrations and protests, consumed with the desire to be a warrior for justice.

After the first year up north, I returned home during the summer of 1963 to participate in nonviolence training and voter registration efforts with the Alabama Christian Movement for Human Rights, a prominent Birmingham civil rights organization that led all the sit-ins, boycotts, litigations, marches, and other militant protests that ultimately brought segregation to its knees. On August 28, 1963, I marched

7

on Washington, D.C., with 250,000 others, calling for jobs, decent housing, civil rights, and an end to police brutality, demands that continue to resonate today, more than fifty-five years later. I remember gazing upon the throngs of young and old, black and white, church folk and trade unionists, and teachers and students. I remember the music along with the beauty and clarity of the light. But mostly, I remember the strong spirit of unity, joy, peace, and victory wafting in the air.

Less than two weeks later, after I had returned to New Jersey as a high school senior, my mother called with devastating news: two close friends had perished in the 1963 Birmingham Sunday School bombing at the Sixteenth Street Baptist Church, an attack carried out by white supremacists to terrorize the rising civil rights movement.

For days, I was angry. Then, numb. Ultimately, the deaths of my friends and other formative experiences stoked inner fires of an enduring commitment to fundamental social change and a deep yearning for freedom for my people from the spirit-crushing systems of racial inequality and terror. Ever since, my life has been a quest for social transformation. For the next decades, I followed the way of the warrior as an activist in the black student, black nationalist, womens', prisoners', anti-imperialist, anti-apartheid, anti-war, anti–racial violence, and socialist movements.

I began undergraduate studies at Swarthmore College in Pennsylvania during the heady days of the black power movement. Critical of the perceived assimilationist stance of the civil rights movement, the youth-driven black power movement emphasized militance and the creation of parallel political and

8

cultural institutions to advance black values and collective economic interests. We unapologetically affirmed blackness. I wore my hair naturally in an "Afro," took an African name, and, for a time, shared antiwhite sentiment. I was active in the Swarthmore African American Students' Association (SASS). In conjunction with the black student protests sweeping the nation in 1968, SASS occupied the Swarthmore admissions office for eight days, demanding better representation of African Americans among students, staff, and faculty, and within the curriculum. The occupation was complicated by the tragic fatal heart attack of the sitting president of the college. But, ultimately, the protest transformed the face of the college, which, by the next year, had more black students, faculty, and administrators. The college also established a black cultural center.

In the heat of the struggle, I married a fellow student leader and activist from a nearby black students' association that worked in solidarity with our group. After graduating, we moved to California in 1969 to begin graduate studies at the University of California, San Diego (UCSD), where my sister was already enrolled. We encountered a campus deep in political turmoil. Throngs of striking students congregated on the campus plaza, demanding that a new school on the UCSD campus be named for Argentinian and Congolese revolutionaries Che Guevara and Patrice Lumumba and that its curriculum equip black and brown students with the knowledge needed to win their peoples' liberation. UCSD students were also engaged in anti–Vietnam War protests, part of the larger student movement then sweeping the nation. We became involved in these efforts and began community-based work with the local Black Panther Party chapter. I also became active in the Soledad Brothers Defense Committee[1] (SBDC) and in the women's liberation movement.

However, barely six months after our arrival, officers broke into our apartment with guns drawn. When my husband went for his gun in self-defense, police shot and nearly killed him. Subsequently, we were both indicted for attempted murder of the very police officers who attacked us. A defense committee sprang into action, raising funds to defray legal costs. Following a long legal battle, charges were finally dismissed when the court ruled we had been targeted for political activism, in violation of the constitution.

During this time, my sister, Angela, was also in news headlines when Ronald Reagan, as the governor of California, fired her from her UCLA teaching position because of her Communist Party membership. The action was overruled as an unlawful violation of her First Amendment rights, and the court ordered reinstatement. The story was widely publicized, and overnight, Angela became a controversial public figure. Faced with countless death threats, she had to surround herself with armed guards at all times, be it at school, protests, or home. But her security detail could not protect her from what happened next.

On August 7, 1970, seventeen-year-old Jonathan Jackson, one of Angela's bodyguards, smuggled guns into a Marin County, California, courtroom, took over the courtroom, and freed three inmates. In the process, he took a judge, district attorney, and three jurors hostage. Outside, they entered an awaiting van, but before Jonathan could drive off, sheriff's deputies fired a hail of bullets into the van, killing the judge, two prisoners, and Jonathan and wounding others. Jonathan brandished guns registered in Angela's name, and, though she was nowhere near the scene and no other evidence linked her to the incident, she was charged with capital murder, kidnapping, and conspiracy. Fearing for her life, having witnessed so many murders of her Black Panther comrades, Angela went underground.

The FBI put her on the Ten Most Wanted list and launched a manhunt unprecedented in scope, involving sweeps and detentions throughout the nation of thousands of light-skinned black women with natural hair styles resembling Angela's. Authorities placed me under personal surveillance, and wherever I went, the shadow of men in suits and ties in unmarked dark cars lurked nearby. A week or so after the incident, a phalanx of SWAT (Special Weapons and Tactics) police officers invaded the San Francisco headquarters for the Soledad Brothers Defense Committee, where I was visiting. Assault guns at the ready, they surrounded me, ready to take me down, until they realized I was not Angela. I was shaken to the core but did my best to hide it as they interrogated me. I was most grateful that it was me at the end of the barrel of those guns, not my sister.

The raid happened when my husband and I were en route to Canada to board a ship bound for Cuba for two months, with hundreds of other members of the third Venceremos Brigade, to plant fruit trees in solidarity with the Cuban Revolution. Once there, we met revolutionaries from around the world, but, despite fervent hopes, I did not find my sister there. Days before returning home, however, we received news that the FBI had captured Angela and taken her into custody, unharmed. In my early twenties at the time, I only wanted one thing—to save my sister's life. My first act when returning from Cuba was to head to New York to visit her in jail. There was a warrant out for my husband's arrest too, related to politically motivated charges of possession of explosives. He surrendered himself to authorities after getting off the boat. My husband would be released in eighteen months, but Angela's life itself was at risk—Governor Reagan, President Nixon, and FBI Director J. Edgar Hoover were intent on silencing her through a legal lynching. Remaining by her side in New York, I began public speaking and giving media interviews.

Within a few months, Angela was extradited to Northern California. I followed. There, I worked closely with seasoned and skilled African American community organizers in the Communist Party to build the National United Committee to Free Angela Davis. The Party activated its extensive international network of skilled community and labor organizers to organize many demonstrations and defense committees. I traveled nationally to speak at mass meetings and demonstrations calling for Angela's freedom. Angela Davis Defense Committees sprang up all over the nation. In people's homes, her photo adorned living room walls, alongside those of Dr. King and President Kennedy. Celebrated artists wrote songs and poems and produced plays and films for Angela. European schoolchildren in communist Germany launched massive letter-writing campaigns; every day, postal carriers would haul bags filled with thousands of letters into Angela's cell. This was the power of the people writ large. I had already considered myself a socialist but was so impressed by the passion, theory, practice, and organizing skills of the black communists who led the campaign to free my sister that I joined the Communist Party.

Shortly after giving birth to my daughter, Angela Eisa, in 1971, I embarked on a speaking tour of dozens of cities in Western and Eastern Europe, the Soviet Union, and Chile, building the international mass movement to save Angela's life. On June 4, 1972, following eighteen months of incarceration, four months of a hard-fought trial, and thirteen hours of deliberation, an all-white jury returned a verdict of not guilty on charges of murder, kidnapping, and criminal conspiracy, fully acquitting my sister. Heartrending screams and shouts tore through the courtroom as the clerk of the court read the verdict and the judge struggled to regain control. The impact of the powerful and massive international movement demanding freedom for Angela was not lost on us that day.

After three more years of organizing around political prisoners and economic justice in the Bay Area, I entered law school, convinced a law degree would make me a more effective agent of social transformation. While in law school, I helped lead a campaign to defend affirmative action and another to challenge the decision to deny tenure to a radical black professor. As I started to practice law, I also became active in anti-apartheid solidarity movements and efforts to stem the rise of the Ku Klux Klan and other racial terrorist groups at home. For more than twenty-five years, I was a trial lawyer, specializing in employment discrimination litigation, with a subspecialty in academic employment discrimination, mostly challenging discriminatory tenure denials by colleges and universities.

After nearly three decades of cultivating the hyper-aggressive, hyperrational, and hyper-masculinist personal qualities needed to be an effective activist and civil rights litigator, I fell out of balance. I was diagnosed with a precancerous condition. Transformation beckoned. Dreams, intuition, and my body were inviting me to summon more creative, healing, and spiritual energies into my life. I answered the call and shut down my law office to pursue a PhD in indigenous studies, a program in which I traveled to Africa to recover my indigenous origins and live with and learn from African traditional healers.

Shortly after returning from Africa and completing the PhD, I learned about restorative justice—a justice that seeks not to punish, but to heal. A justice, according to Kay Pranis, that is not about getting even, but about getting well.[2] A justice that seeks to transform broken lives, relationships, and communities, rather than shatter them further. A justice that seeks reconciliation, rather than a deepening of conflict. A healing justice rather than a harming justice. Learning about this new but ancient justice marked a climax in my own years-long movement toward wholeness. It provoked an epiphany, integrating my inner warrior with my inner healer and uniting the opposites within: fire/water, solar/lunar, and masculine/feminine. Restorative justice allowed me to integrate these hitherto disparate parts. I did not have to choose one and renounce the other. At last, I could be all of me.

A primary purpose of this book is to invite restorative justice practitioners to cultivate a heightened racial justice consciousness and racial justice activists to embrace a greater healing consciousness. Through

14

the coupling of what I refer to as "warrior" and "healer," we develop the capacity to fulfill the promise of both the racial justice and restorative justice movements—disrupt the school-to-prison pipeline, interrupt the "New Jim Crow" of mass incarceration, transform the historical harm that drives present-day state-sanctioned police violence against people of color, and ultimately, in my view, take the next step on the evolutionary journey of reimagining what it means to be human.

Chapter 2 reviews the fundamentals of restorative justice, exposes its indigenous roots, and illustrates African-centered justice approaches. Through a critical race theory lens, Chapter 3 examines the nature of race and racism in the United States, the dearth of racial justice consciousness during the first forty years of the restorative justice movement, and the dynamic transformations currently underway. Chapter 4 addresses the school-to-prison pipeline and race-based restorative justice practices in schools, with examples from Oakland, California, and Denver, Colorado, schools. Chapter 5 addresses the origins of the US punishment system in slavery, its afterlife in the form of racialized mass incarceration, and how prison activists and restorative justice practitioners are responding to it. Chapter 6 envisions a homegrown restorative justice–based truth and reconciliation process to transform police violence against African Americans. Chapter 7 reviews the unprecedented truth-telling efforts bubbling up across the nation today, outlines the evolution of my notion of justice over my life's journey, and concludes with an exhortation to activists and restorative justice practitioners to live and work at the intersection of healing and activism. The start of each chapter is adorned with an Adinkra image, visual symbols encoding proverbs and aphorisms of the Akan people, a large ethnic group of present-day Ghana and the Ivory Coast, West Africa.

The focus on antiblack racism in this Little Book is not meant to deny or minimize the existence of anti-Latinx, anti–Native American, anti–Asian American, and other racisms. Indeed, other racialized histories have informed the development of both the criminal justice and restorative justice in the United States. This book, however, is meant to explore the black experience, not in a narrow nationalistic exercise, but in a way that teases out implications for how we might collectively forge a transformed and just future for all.

2.
Ubuntu: The Indigenous Ethos of Restorative Justice

SANKOFA

The bird looks backward to bring forth the seed of a new future. Let us go back to the past to fetch that which is useful for the future.

Umuntu, ngumuntu, ngabantu.

This Nguni proverb, translated as "I am because we are and we are because I am," expresses the universal African core belief that the individual exists only in relationship to the collective. This communitarian view is known as *ubuntu* in southern Africa's

Zulu, Xhosa, Tswana, Venda, and other African traditions. Also translated to mean "a person is a person through their relationships," *ubuntu* emphasizes humans' interidentity and interrelationality with all dimensions of existence—other people, places, land, animals, waters, air, and so on. *Ubuntu* affirms not only our inherent interrelatedness, but also the resulting responsibility we bear to one another, flowing precisely from our deep connection. As the Lakota Sioux put it, *"Mitákuye Oyás'iŋ,"* we are all relatives; we are here on earth to learn to take care of one another. As relatives living within the continuum of creation, it is our responsibility to live in "right relationship" and be present to one another and to the earth in ways that promote healing and flourishing for all.

Neither tyranny of community nor extreme individualism, *ubuntu* invokes a dialectical unity of opposites. In the African worldview,[1] independence is inseparable from interdependence, and individuality expands from being solitary to being in solidarity. Morality, fairness, and justice are not narrowly construed, based on the primacy of individual rights, but rather based on a strong sense of one's connection and responsibility to others.[2] "*Ubuntu* unites the self and the world in a . . . web of reciprocal relations."[3] It is one's caring relationship with others that enhances their humanity and self-worth.[4]

Popularized by Archbishop Desmond Tutu and Nelson Rolilhalha Mandela, *ubuntu* became part of the international lexicon during the transition from apartheid to Western democracy in South Africa in the mid-1990s. It served as the philosophical cornerstone of South Africa's internationally renowned restorative justice–based truth and reconciliation process.

18

Restorative justice pioneer Howard Zehr links restorative justice to the Judeo-Christian concept of *shalom*, which "[e]mphasiz[es] 'right relationships' between individuals, between groups of people, between people and the earth, and between people and the divine [and] declares an allegiance to respecting life in all its forms. . . . [It] encourages us to see the nurturing of this sacred relational web as our ultimate calling."[5]

Consonant with African and other indigenous communitarian values, restorative justice (RJ) is profoundly relational and emphasizes bringing together everyone affected by wrongdoing to address needs and responsibilities and to heal the harm to relationships and community, to the degree possible. While often mistakenly considered only a reactive response to harm, restorative justice is also a proactive relational strategy to create a culture of connectivity where all members of a community thrive and feel valued.

Indigenous Wisdom and Justice

While the emergence of US restorative justice in the late 1970s did not explicitly acknowledge indigeneity as its birthright—African or otherwise—this began to shift around the turn of the century.[6] Chief Justice Emeritus of the Navajo Nation Supreme Court Robert Yazzie has been speaking and writing about Navajo restorative justice since the 1980s. Since the 1990s, Dr. Morris Jenkins has been researching and publishing about the African-centered justice practices of the Gullah, an African-descended people living in the Carolinas, Georgia, and Sea Islands who preserved and today still practice African lifeways. Having revived traditional peacemaking circles and successfully collaborated with Judge Barry Stuart in their use in Yukon criminal sentencing processes, Harold and Phil Gatensby and Chief Mark Wedge of the Tglingit First Nations were also key to the dissemination of the peacemaking circle process across the United States and Canada in their role as initial trainers. Kay Pranis's *The Little Book of Circle Processes* affirms and explores the indigenous teachings and values that comprise the foundations of the circle process and of restorative justice more broadly. Pranis acknowledges it was the Tlingit and Tagish people of Canada who taught her—and authorized her to teach—the peacemaking circle process.[7] The indigenous roots of restorative justice refer not just to the origins of the circle technique, says Pranis, but perhaps "more importantly, the roots are in the world view of indigenous people—the understanding of interconnectedness and the dignity of all parts of creation . . . [This is] an evolving concept . . . [that] has grown in importance over the years."[8]

It is noted that to emphasize the indigenous ethos of restorative justice is not to sanction cultural appropriation. If restorative justice facilitators seek to incorporate indigenous elements of another culture in their circle practice, for example, respect requires, at minimum, fully understanding and explaining to circle participants the meaning of the cultural practice and identifying the individual who shared it and authorized them to use it. That said, every human being has indigenous roots, including white people, and all restorative justice practitioners might consider unearthing the healing and peacemaking ceremonies and practices of their own ancestral traditions to incorporate into their restorative justice practice.

Resurgence of Indigenous Knowledges

Etymologically, the word "indigenous" arises out of the Latin *indo* and Greek *endina*, referring to emergence from the very entrails of a place. *Gen* connotes birth and *geni,* spirit. Indigenous then refers to beings, worldviews, values, ways of life, and ways of knowing engendered from and belonging to a land that existed before the *conquista* and colonization. Indigenous peoples and worldviews are by no means homogenous. However, their axiologies, cosmologies, epistemologies, and ontologies[9] bear striking resemblances across infinitely diverse geographies and cultural expressions worldwide.

Contemporary restorative justice arises alongside the historical backdrop of heightened international awareness that indigenous knowledges, grounded in an ecological ethos of interrelatedness and collaboration, have much to offer today's fractured world. The corollary is the growing recognition that for more than five hundred years, Western knowledge systems, based on an ethos of separateness, competition, and subordination, have contributed to pervasive crises that today imperil our future. The scale of devastation is unprecedented—whether of our bodies, families, and communities, or plants, animals, waters, and earth. The unfathomable magnitude of the destruction has fueled a quest for alternative worldviews that bring healing to our world. It is in this historical context that we witness the rapid global rise and spread of restorative justice.

Today's resurgence of indigenous wisdom fulfills prophecy. During the 1500s, Native American elders gathered in Mexico as they faced the early days of the onslaught of European colonization. Through

21

their ancient scientific practices, Cuauthemoc, the great Aztec ruler, recognized humanity was entering a "Dark Sun," which would continue for almost five hundred years, at the end of which we would enter a "Bright Sun" of human consciousness. The elders prophesied that the condor, signifying the South and feminine and lunar energies, would fly together with the eagle, representing the North and masculine and solar energies. They predicted that in the time of the Bright Sun, the two would reunite and the ancient knowledge of the earth would reemerge from all the four directions.[10]

Indeed, almost five hundred years ago, numerous global events portended the Dark Sun of human consciousness—for example, the rise of the Papal Doctrine of Discovery, which sanctioned the conquest and subjugation of indigenous peoples throughout the world, the rise of the international slave trade, the genocide of Native Americans, individualism, materialism, the emergence of racial capitalism (to be explored in Chapter 5), and the very notion of race itself. However, today, according to prophecy, we are moving out of the Dark Sun. The rapid rise and growth of restorative justice manifests the larger phenomenon of a resurgence of indigenous wisdom.

Restorative Justice and African Indigenous Justice

In the African-centered view, human beings are by nature good. African humanism affirms the inherent goodness and equal moral worth and dignity of all. By contrast, some Judeo-Christian perspectives, even with the concept of *shalom*, hold that humans are by nature sinful, though with religion can be redeemed.

Because European colonialists saw no jails, police, lawyers, judges, or courts in African indigenous societies, they mistakenly concluded these cultures had no way to address social conflict and wrongdoing. Without such institutions to restrain human nature, they believed these cultures were inherently unstable, brutish, and chaotic in the Hobbesian sense.[11] However, invisible to the eyes searching for a justice system based upon rule of law and punishment was a deeply held worldview affirming the interrelatedness of all life as well as countless social institutions, cultural bonds, and practices that gave life, on a daily basis, to that strongly held sense of oneness and community—e.g., ceremony, initiation age-group linkages, and secret societies, as well as intermarriage and joking relationships that united different ethnic groups, lineages, clans, and villages, thus making spilling of blood among them taboo. Powerful communal bonds, woefully lacking in contemporary culture, are a community's greatest security and protection from crime.

Though inherently good in the African-centered view, humans make mistakes. Yet, they are capable of learning and changing. African justice making, rather than an occasion to inflict punishment, is an opportunity to teach, learn, reemphasize social values, and reaffirm the bonds of our inherent interrelatedness. It is also an opportunity to identify and redress problematic social conditions that may have given rise to interpersonal harm.[12]

In African indigenous justice, vindication of the person harmed is prioritized. The person responsible, and often their family, is obligated to offer apology, recompense, and reparation to the harmed person and community. A wrong can be made right by subsequent actions of the responsible person and other community members. Community is central. The concept of family in Africa embraces the nuclear family and the extended family as well as people who do not share blood or marriage relationships. Also, the African family extends beyond the living to include the realm of the ancestors.

Indeed, in the African worldview, when something happens to one, whether blessing or burden, it happens to all. A newborn baby is good fortune for family and also the entire village. Marriage unites two clans, not just two individuals. The deeply communal ethos among African and other indigenous traditions also holds true when wrongdoing occurs. If an individual steals from or kills another, they damage the relationship between their respective lineages or villages. In the wake of harm, making it right is not solely the responsibility of the individuals directly involved; it is also the responsibility of communities. The focus is on repairing and rebuilding relationships with the intent of bringing social harmony. African indigenous justice seeks to strengthen relationships by fashioning win-win outcomes.

In keeping with the worldview and principles of African and other indigenous justice systems, restorative justice invites a paradigm shift in the way we think about and do justice—from a justice that harms to a justice that heals. Our prevailing adversarial system is based upon a Roman notion of justice as just deserts. Causing someone to suffer creates an imbalance in the scales of justice, and the way to rebalance the scales and do justice is to cause the responsible person to suffer; we respond to the original harm with a second harm. Ours is a system that harms people who harm people, presumably to show that harming people is wrong. This sets into motion endless cycles of harm. Restorative justice seeks to interrupt these cycles by repairing the damage done to relationships in the wake of crime or other wrongdoing, and do so in a way that is consonant with indigenous wisdom—Africa's and that of other traditions. Justice is a healing ground, not a battleground.

In Western culture, we are socialized to believe that the desire to inflict counterviolence upon or retaliate against someone who has hurt us or a loved one is innate and that justice has always been done and will always be done in this way. In fact, far from universal or natural, this adversarial vision of justice is a relatively recent cultural and historical construction, arising around AD 1200 with the dawning of the nation-state and racial capitalism. Though restorative justice is new to Western jurisprudence, it is not at all new in the broader sweep of human history. For most of human history, reconciliation and restitution to victims and their kin took precedence over vengeance. This is because restoring social peace and avoiding blood feuds were paramount social concerns. Restitution and reconciliation, not punishment, were overarching aspirations.

Indeed, in most indigenous languages, there is no word for prison. If you stole something or hurt someone, then family members would pay restitution—for instance, in Africa, with maize, palm oil, chickens, goats, or cows—and exert a corrective influence. Your wrongdoing, the act, is shamed, not you. Family urges you to empathize with the person you harmed, acknowledge the wrong, apologize, make amends, and ask forgiveness. Even murder was not punishable by death in most societies before AD 1200. For instance, in ancient Zimbabwe, if you killed someone, you would pay 109 goats. If you had no goats, you would offer one of your children to the victim's family. If you did not have a child, an adult from your family would go live with the dead person's family. Though the family expected the new addition to serve them, that individual was accepted and free to marry into the new family and pursue a livelihood like everyone else. Indigenous justice focuses on repairing and rebuilding in order to strengthen relationships and bring social harmony.

African indigenous justice scholar Ocho Elechi notes that African indigenous justice processes continue to be widely used in Africa today, often alongside modern Western justice practices. Elechi attributes the lower crime and incarceration rates in most African countries, compared to such rates in Western nations, to the greater effectiveness of African indigenous justice processes.[13]

While our modern Eurocentric justice framework focuses tightly on the individual causing harm, restorative justice, consistent with indigenous justice, expresses a more expansive and communal concern by focusing on the needs and responsibilities of those causing harm, those directly harmed, and all other affected persons and communities. Attention to the entire collective distinguishes restorative justice as a communal, holistic, and balanced justice.

Restorative justice provides an opportunity for those who harm and those harmed to empathize with one another, rather than foster hostility between them and their communities. It encourages the responsible person and the community, where appropriate, to take responsibility for actions resulting in harm and make amends. Restorative justice processes invite individuals and the community to take steps to prevent recurrence. Ultimately, it offers processes where the person harmed and all impacted parties can begin to heal.

Criminal justice sees crime as broken laws and justice as punishment. It intentionally pits two opposing parties against each other in a zero-sum battle to determine right/wrong, guilt/innocence, and winner/loser. Restorative justice sees crime as broken lives and justice as healing. And there are no sides. Parties enter into the justice process, together focused on accountability and the common central question: how do we heal and transform relationships and structures in the wake of harm? To the degree possible, restorative justice seeks a healing for all versus a victory for one. This frequently occurs through a threefold collaborative and dialogical process: (1) storytelling and relationship building, (2) truth-telling and accountability, and (3) reparative action. Even when both parties do not meet face-to-face, the restorative justice process seeks to achieve these three elements.

Restorative justice elevates the voices of survivors, families, communities, and responsible parties in ways that rarely occur in the adversarial context and, in doing so, aspires toward greater community self-governance by bringing together all members impacted by wrongdoing to identify harm, assess needs, meet responsibilities, and heal and repair harm to the degree possible. It shifts the locus of the justice project from dependence on systems and professionals to reliance on the involvement of

27

communities and ordinary people. It moves us from an individualist "I" to a communalist "we," thereby strengthening communities. Individual and community safety and security emerge from healthier and self-governing communities, not from more police or prisons.

Restorative justice views a vengeful and punitive response to harm unacceptable, because, on a social level, it sets into motion negative feedback loops of violence and counterviolence. Punishment, the equivalent of officially sanctioned vengeance, is a mere variant of the original harm, replicating and reproducing it, resulting in the destruction of community safety nets and social breakdown. An eye for an eye and a tooth for a tooth leaves the whole world blind and toothless. On an individual level, a punitive, vengeful response harms us psychologically. It locks us into the past and tethers us to disabling definitions of ourselves and an overidentification with the pain, mistaking it for who we truly are. This attachment to suffering blocks the path to healing, magnifies vengeance, and expands pain. Imprisoned by the pain and the past, the harmed party experiences victimization a second time, but this time, it is self-inflicted. It is scientifically documented that hatred and anger eat away at our well-being, on physical and emotional levels.

This is not to say that persons harmed must forgive; it is rather an invitation to transform punitive and vengeful responses. It is important that survivors feel no pressure to forgive; coercion has no place in restorative justice processes. Contrary to popular notions that conflate forgiveness with restorative justice, forgiveness is neither required nor guaranteed in restorative justice processes. Nor is it a determinant of success. Success happens in well-prepared and well-facilitated encounters where persons who have been harmed feel safe enough to freely share their stories and express their needs and persons causing harm tell the truth, express remorse and responsibility, and offer reparations. Success continues when all participants together fashion a plan to repair harm that is actually carried out. This may—or may not—lead to forgiveness. Either way, restorative justice has done its job.

Ultimately, restorative justice signifies the dawning of a new justice, a Bright Sun, that transcends the punitive and narrow assumptions of prevailing justice and offers a broader view of justice inspired by indigenous values. That is, a new but old justice that is healing, relational, community-based, inclusivist, participatory, needs- and accountability-based, and forward-looking.

3.
Integrating Racial Justice and Restorative Justice

FUNTUMFUNAFU DENKYEMFUNAFU

These conjoined crocodiles frequently quarrel when they eat together though they have a shared stomach. Let us stop quarreling; our common destiny unites us.

As I learned more about restorative justice, the large number of books, papers, and essays on the subject was astonishing. Not surprisingly given my lifelong journey as a racial justice activist, I was particularly interested in exploring the intersection of racial and restorative justice. A Google search, however, turned up not even a handful of publications addressing race, whiteness, the civil rights movement, mass incarceration, or the overrepresentation of persons of color in the criminal justice system.

Nor had there been any conferences or other gatherings on the subject. The restorative justice movement appeared to have no racial justice consciousness!

The following overview of the nature and history of race and racism in the United States sheds light on why the restorative justice community has failed to address race. This chapter also urges us to see restorative justice as a social movement, not solely as social services, and concludes with reflections on the importance of race in the restorative justice movement and of healing in the racial justice movement. Though we are seeing glimmers of change, racial justice and restorative justice are often perceived as opposites. In archetypal terms, one invokes the warrior and the other, the healer. If we are to be as transformative as possible, however, whether as racial justice or restorative justice advocates, we must transcend the binary and integrate warrior and healer.

Race and Racism in the United States

The United States is a nation born in the blood of the enslavement of Africans and genocide of Native Americans. It is founded on white supremacy, the bedrock belief that the white race is inherently superior to the black race. Yet race has no biological or genetic basis; the nation deliberately constructed this pseudoscientific notion to justify slavery's unspeakable terrors. "White" people and "black" people are historico-social inventions. Neither the people nor designations existed before slavery.

Race is not real, but racism is very real. We are a nation that is loath to confront and be honest about the meaning of slavery, genocide, lynching, segregation, mass incarceration, and the unremitting torrent

31

of racist abuse against communities of color. Though slavery was legally abolished in the nineteenth century, as were convict leasing and Jim Crow in the twentieth, the racial terror and white supremacy at their essence live on today in the form of racialized mass incarceration and police brutality. They live on when the forty-fifth president calls Confederate monuments "beautiful," refers to El Salvador, Haiti, and African countries as "shitholes," and creates a false moral equivalence between violent Ku Klux Klanners and Neo-Nazis on one hand and protestors acting in self-defense on the other. The centuries-long failure to confront this history dooms us perpetually to repeat it. Our failure to reckon with the past precludes our ability to take collective responsibility, transform relationships and social structures, and finally put the past behind us.

Americans are socialized to reduce racism to individual expressions of prejudice and overt acts of bigotry. Yet racism in the United States is three-dimensional: structural, institutional, and individual (see page 34: Figure 1). *Structural racism* is the normalization and legitimization of white supremacy, enacted from the nation's beginnings, by vast historical, governmental, cultural, economic, educational, institutional, and psychological forces, all working in concert to perpetuate racial inequity. These forces collude to create an absolute system of unequal power that privileges white skin and disadvantages black skin, a system that persists undiminished in potency through time. Structural racism cannot easily be located in any particular practice or institution because it saturates and pervades all: "it reinforce[s] . . . effects of multiple institutions and cultural norms, past and present, continually producing new, and re-producing old forms of racism."[1]

Institutional racism involves the ubiquitous practices and policies within schools, workplaces, financial establishments, housing, hospitals, the justice system, and other private and governmental institutions that, intentionally or not, produce outcomes that consistently advantage whites while disadvantaging people of color. Examples are policies resulting in redlining, the school-to-prison pipeline, mass incarceration, police killings, and enduring disparities in life spans, health, and wealth.

Individual racism encompasses the explicit or implicit racial bias that plays out in interpersonal spheres. Though in the Trump era we see a burgeoning of overt racism (e.g., an increase in hate crimes[2]), contemporary individual racism mostly manifests as implicit bias occurring when a person rejects stereotypes on conscious levels yet holds onto them on unconscious levels. Implicit bias is more insidious than explicit bias because it drives our behavior while we are completely unaware. For example, "shooter studies" show police tend to be quicker to associate blackness than whiteness with guilt and consequently are more likely to make split-second decisions to use deadly force against blacks than whites.[3]

In general, more than 85 percent of all Americans view themselves as unbiased, yet studies show that most Americans have implicit bias.[4] One study found that 80 percent of whites and 40 percent of blacks have a prowhite bias, consistently showing blacks are associated with such negative stereotypes as bad, lazy, aggressive, and unpleasant.[5] When historically marginalized people have implicit bias, it is often referred to as internalized oppression.[6]

The common view that a black individual expressing antiwhite sentiment can be just as racist as a white individual expressing antiblack animus is mistaken. Because it is backed up by nearly four hundred years of structural and institutional power, antiblack racism is more potent and virulent by several orders of magnitude; there is no comparison.

Figure 1.

3 TYPES OF RACISM

STRUCTURAL RACISM
Normalization and legitimization of white supremacy from the nation's beginnings enacted by historical, institutional and cultural forces working in tandem.

INSTITUTIONAL RACISM
Policies and practices of private and governmental institutions that produce outcomes that consistently advantage whites while disadvantaging people of color; i.e., mass incarceration, school-to-prison pipeline and widening health, wealth, education, and housing disparities.

INDIVIDUAL RACISM
Explicit or implicit racial bias by dominant group individuals. (This also includes a person of color's internalized oppression.)

Restorative justice exists within and is informed by racist structures, institutions, and individual bias. Structural racism is not something present-day white people chose or created. They benefit from it, however, and are responsible for changing it, because the status quo is racism. Good intentions notwithstanding, doing nothing about racism necessarily reproduces it; to fail to take action is to be complicit.

Restorative Justice as a Social Movement

I have always viewed restorative justice as a social movement—a loosely organized but sustained collective effort comprised of a range of individuals and groups seeking to transform social structures, institutions, and individuals. Healing interpersonal harm requires a commitment to transforming the context in which the injury occurs: the socio-historical conditions and institutions that are structured precisely to perpetuate harm. This commitment may mean viewing restorative justice as not only healing individual harm, but also as transforming social structures and institutions that are themselves purveyors of massive harm. Not adopting a more expansive view runs the risk that restorative justice offers a quick fix, addressing symptoms but not underlying causes. This is not unlike a gardener who, though devoted to the well-being of the individual plants, ignores the health of the soil. The skilled gardener tends to both plants and the larger ecosystem. The success of restorative justice depends on seeing ourselves not only as agents of individual transformation, but also as drivers of systems transformation.

Significantly, restorative justice actually arises out of and is heir to a number of social movements, including the victims' rights, feminist, mediation, prison abolitionist, and peace movements. It shares a special kinship with the civil rights movement and its spiritual grounding in principles of nonviolence, ahimsa,[7] satyagraha,[8] truth-telling, and engaging the enemy with compassion. Restorative justice is consistent with Dr. King's vision of justice as "love correcting that which revolts against love."

Race and Social Movements

The lack of racial justice consciousness within the restorative justice community is the direct result of structural and institutional racism and part of an entrenched historical pattern: with the exception of movements initiated by people of color, all social movements in the United States have started out virtually all-white and have failed to engage issues of race, particularly in their early decades. The racist and elitist biases of the women's movement, for instance, were exposed and denounced by Sojourner Truth, Frederick Douglass, and, later, the Third World Women's Alliance, Angela Davis, and Black Lives Matter. We are now seeing change. The historic 2017 Women's March carried a consistent message, albeit only after women of color intervened, that current social issues, in addition to equal pay and reproductive rights, are *all* women's issues—e.g., mass incarceration, police killings, transphobia, Islamophobia, xenophobia, the environment and water, the occupation of Palestine, and economic justice. The victims' rights movement is also changing. Crime Survivors for Safety and Justice, Common Justice, and others are challenging racial stereotypes that portray persons harmed as white people and persons causing harm as people of color. These transformations in the women's and victims' rights movements signal the emergence of a more intersectional consciousness and heightened awareness about racial and social justice within activist spaces.

We see a similar pattern within the restorative justice movement. In 2011, a small group of restorative justice practitioners and I gathered, discussed the troubling whiteness of the restorative justice movement, and resolved to take action. This culminated in the first national restorative justice conference (2013) featuring race and restorative justice as the theme and a dialogue between racial and restorative justice advocates. In the years since, convenings, research, publications, and curricula increasingly address racial equity. A dramatic embodiment of this transformation was the 2017 national conference, cohosted by Restorative Justice Oakland Youth (RJOY; Oakland, CA), which centered historically marginalized voices in the areas of race, gender, gender expression, age, class, religion, and incarcerated and immigration status. It is no coincidence that much of the transformative impulse originated from Oakland, the birthplace of the Black Panther Party, an iconic racial and social justice organization founded in 1966. Today, some fifty years later, Oakland is a flourishing restorative justice site where people practice restorative justice through a social and racial justice lens while honoring its indigenous roots.

Race Matters in Restorative Justice Practice

Restorative justice risks losing relevance if we, as practitioners, do not become more skillful at identifying, navigating, and transforming racial harm. Structural racism pervades all our institutions, meaning race matters whether we work in schools, criminal justice, the workplace, or the community. Further, the 2015 US Census projects that more than half of all children under eighteen will be members of racial minorities by 2020 and, by 2044, white Americans will no longer constitute the majority. Yet, by every measure, stark racial inequities persist.[9]

Given the nation's changing demographics and persistent, if not deepening, racial disparities, a restorative justice approach that ignores these inequities will be perceived as uninformed and uncaring, if not irrelevant and racist. Failing to acknowledge and take action to address racial injustice allows living legacies of slavery, genocide, and segregation to persist. With the heightened awareness of police terror against people of color and the resurgence of white hate crimes, we are having a dramatic lived experience of this truth.

Healing Matters in Racial Justice Movements

Just as restorative justice advocates have historically ignored race, racial justice activists, including myself in the past, have disregarded the need for healing on individual and collective levels. This is beginning to change, however. Grace Lee Boggs, one of the nation's great freedom fighters, left a legacy of radical social activism inspired by spirituality. Another celebrated freedom fighter, Ella Jo Baker, believed that movement leaders could not critique elitism and hierarchy in society while emulating these same values in their movement organizations and personal lives. This theme is picked up by today's black youth activists, who are less binary, and more loving and compassionate, in their ways of being present to one another and the Earth than earlier generations.

This is perhaps most clearly evident in the Black Lives Matter (BLM) network, emerging after the 2012 death of Trayvon Martin and rapidly spreading with the 2014 killing of Michael Brown. BLM's guiding principles include a commitment to "restorative justice," working "lovingly . . . [to] nurture a beloved community," and "practicing empathy . . . justice, liberation, and peace in our engagements with one another." They aim to elevate historically marginalized voices, particularly those of queer, trans, undocumented, and disabled brothers and sisters, and create "extended families and 'villages' that collectively care for one another," especially the children. These beautifully expressed principles demonstrate a heightened awareness of the importance of doing the internal work of transforming self while transforming the world.[10]

While these laudable aspirations express the views of BLM's founding leadership and not necessarily those of the totality of this decentralized movement, they are a far cry from my experience as someone involved in successive waves of activism from the 1960s through the 1990s. Then, the words *love, empathy,* and *nurturance* were not only absent from our lexicon, they were disdained. Hypermasculinity, hyper-rationality, militance, toughness, and "revolutionary rage" were exalted. Spirituality was taboo, violative of fundamental Marxist and dialectical materialist tenets. I tried to hide my spiritual, meditative, and yoga practices in those days, but comrades who managed to discover them made me the butt of jokes and ridicule.

As participants in the peace movement during the Vietnam War, my peers and I did not cultivate peace in our relations with one another. Though public proponents of equality, we created hierarchies within our organizations. Our male cisgendered leaders were sexist, too often relegating women to the sidelines. We were socialized in modernist, colonized ways of thinking, being, and knowing, espousing either/or, right/wrong, and other binaries that create division instead of wholeness. Though we verbally affirmed the need for collective strategizing, leadership, and action, in actuality we were often individualistic and ego-based in our interactions, leading to internecine conflict that, spurred on by agents provocateurs, sometimes became lethal.

Today, the BLM movement, including groups like Black Youth Project 100, leads the way in this emerging trend toward more relational, holistic, and creative approaches to activism and helps to catalyze dramatic anti-racist transformations throughout the nation. However, a commitment to radical healing (e.g., self-healing, trauma healing, community healing, trans-racial healing, and healing historical harms) is largely still missing from most racial and social justice projects.

Healing is so important for us in this nation. We have historically sought justice with varying degrees of success. We succeeded in abolishing slavery, yet the racial terror that was the essence of slavery survived and continued with the convict leasing system, Jim Crow, and lynching. Though we passed laws to abolish these aftermaths of slavery, they remain today, having morphed into racialized mass incarceration and police terror. Indeed, even the affirmation that black lives matter is not new. During the early 1800s, the abolitionist symbol was a black man on his knees in chains with writing circling over his head: "Am I Not a Man and a Brother?" This was a catchphrase abolitionists used again during the struggle around the Supreme Court's Dred Scott decision in the mid-1800s. During the civil rights era at the Memphis Sanitation Strike in 1968, "I AM A MAN!" signs again sought to affirm black humanity. Today, BLM echoes the same theme, albeit with a heightened consciousness around gender and gender expression. Similarly, the Black Panther Party's ten-point program issued more than fifty years ago called for decent housing, income, health care, and education, and an end to police violence, mass incarceration, and unemployment. These very demands were made during the Reconstruction era.[11] They continue to resonate today.

We have reached a historical point in this country where it is clear that if we do not seek both justice and healing, injustice will keep replicating itself ad nauseum and we will find ourselves intoning the very same social justice demands generation after generation. Taken together, restorative justice as a movement conscious of racial justice and social justice as a movement conscious of restorative justice offer a way forward.

4.
Race, Restorative Justice, and Schools

AKONONAN

The hen treads on her chicks but does not kill them. Let us nurture and discipline our children, but not hurt them.

A four-year-old black boy in a California preschool is suspended for theft for retrieving his bag of Skittles that the principal confiscated.

A black seven-year-old special-needs boy is arrested for throwing a tantrum while decorating an Easter egg.

A twelve-year-old Latina girl doodling on her desk is arrested by a NYPD police officer, handcuffed, and perp-walked out of the school for defacing public property.

*A food fight in a middle school cafeteria in
Chicago results in arrests and two-day suspensions
for reckless conduct of twenty-five black children,
ages eleven to fifteen.*

*A fourteen-year-old black boy is arrested on charges of
disorderly conduct and petty larceny for "stealing" a sixty-
five-cent carton of milk, even though he was entitled to
it as a participant in the school's free lunch program.*

*A sixteen-year-old African American honor student is
arrested for possession of a destructive device because
her science experiment went awry, even though it
resulted in no personal harm or property damage.*

*A police officer violently slams a quietly sitting
black girl out of her classroom desk and across
the room because she didn't surrender her cell
phone. A classmate who was recording the incident
with her phone was also arrested.*

"Casserian Njera" is a traditional greeting of the
Maasai people who inhabit Kenya and northern
Uganda. Translated from the Maa language, it means
"How are the children?" On the dusty roads, on the
mountain passes, and in the village marketplaces,
the fabled and fierce Maasai warriors always ask and
answer this question. It is always on their minds, in
their hearts, and floating in the air. As the appalling
true stories above of violence targeting our children
while at school suggest, we have much to learn from
these ancient people about the centrality of a society's responsibility to care for its most defenseless
and vulnerable. These stories are not aberrations;

43

they are products of the structural, institutional, and individual racism on which the United States is founded.

Following an introduction to the importance of education in the liberation of black people, this chapter discusses current zero tolerance school discipline policies and their causes and consequences, particularly for children of color. It surveys the increasing body of evidence showing that school-based restorative justice strategies are successfully transforming zero tolerance discipline and improving educational conditions and outcomes for youth of color. Finally, case studies from Oakland (California) and Denver (Colorado) offer successful examples of how restorative justice can reduce racial disparities in school discipline.

Education as a Liberatory Practice

From slavery times to the present, black people have treasured education as liberatory. It was unlawful for enslaved blacks to learn to read and write. When the slavemaster learned his wife was teaching young Frederick Douglass to read, he at once forbade it: "[I]f you teach . . . [him] how to read, there would be no keeping him. It would forever unfit him to be a slave." Upon hearing these words, Douglass had an epiphany, understanding in that moment that education was "the path way from slavery to freedom" and was the most important thing he and other slaves could do to free themselves. Douglass went on to become a leader in the anti-slavery and women's rights movements, a best-selling author, and a US diplomat.

Author and educator bell hooks continues this black tradition, exhorting educators to enact a revolutionary pedagogy of resistance that is profoundly anticolonial and anti-racist. This is education as the practice of freedom, as famed critical pedagogist Paulo Friere puts it, and it means implementing practices that both challenge curricular and pedagogical biases that reinforce systems of domination like racism and sexism while simultaneously creating innovative ways to teach diverse groups of students. Instead of creating pathways to liberation and opportunity, however, too many schools today are pushing children into pipelines of incarceration and violence.

Zero Tolerance School Discipline

Zero tolerance school policies criminalize children instead of educating them. Creating mandatory punishments, much like the criminal justice system, for certain rule violations, no matter how minor, these punishments often involve arrests, expulsions, or suspensions. Zero tolerance intensified in the wake of the mass shooting at Columbine High School in Colorado in the late 1990s to the point that today, school architecture mimics prison architecture, and the environment is further prison-ized, especially in low-income communities of color, with an increased police presence and surveillance (e.g., use of metal detectors, security cameras, and wand searches). In recent decades, out-of-school suspensions and school-based arrests have become the norm for not only brandishing weapons and assault, but also for talking back to teachers, tardiness, playful adolescent behavior, and even temper tantrums. Over the time in which these policies have been implemented, out-of-school suspensions have increased by 100 percent for all children.

These policies are rationalized as necessary to increase safety and academic achievement, but research and reality belie this. Actually, schools with higher rates of suspensions are neither smarter nor safer than those with lower rates.[1] Time spent learning is one of the strongest predictors of academic and social success. Research shows that removing children from the classroom contributes to missed instructional time, decreased school engagement, and diminished trust between students and adults. It also removes students from adult supervision for extended periods. Further, being suspended once in ninth grade doubles the dropout risk and triples the chance of juvenile justice involvement within one year.[2]

High suspension rates also cost taxpayers billions. According to researchers, suspensions from tenth grade alone led to 67,000 high school dropouts nationwide, resulting over the course of a lifetime in $163,000 in lost tax revenues and $364,000 in other social costs, including health and criminal justice expenses with a cumulative cost exceeding $35 billion.[3]

Racial Disparities

Zero tolerance policies disproportionately impact students of color. African American students are nearly four times as likely as their white classmates to be suspended from school for similar infractions. Black girls are suspended at a rate eight times that of white female peers.[4] Behavioral differences do not explain the disparities. Today, 80 percent of the nation's public school teachers are white, and consequently, implicit bias is thus more likely to occur in public schools with a majority of students of color.

One school study showed that teachers treat African American students less favorably than white students. Another showed a teacher explained a white student's misconduct by reference to external factors, such as family, while viewing a black student's misbehavior as attributable to internal deficits, such as lack of self-control.[5] Implicit bias by individuals in the chain of school discipline decisions, particularly discretionary decisions, produces additional racially disparate outcomes.

The result is that children of color are punished more severely than white children for relatively minor and subjective offenses. The more subjective the category of offense—e.g., insubordination, disobedience, and defiance—the greater the risk that explicit or implicit bias will seep into the discretionary process.[6] Subjected to intersectional forms of stereotyping based on race and gender, such as being "loud" and "ghetto," black girls are especially penalized for deviating from gender norms and expectations of "feminine" behavior, based on models of white womanhood.[7]

Further, the presence of police officers in schools has increased, with the rise of mass incarceration and in the wake of school shootings, to the extent that almost 30 percent of US schools have a police presence, resulting in referrals of hundreds of thousands of children.[8] Putting police in schools criminalizes normal childhood and adolescent behaviors. More and more kids are handcuffed, tased, sprayed, and beaten, not surprisingly, given that police officers are trained to use force and, on average, get 120 hours of training in using force for every eight hours in conflict resolution.[9] Further, it is black students who are

47

most negatively impacted. Nationwide, though they make up only 15.5 percent of overall school enrollees, black students comprise 33.4 percent of students arrested, the worst disparity for any racial group. Moreover, police contact in schools may also have negative immigration consequences for children and their families, triggering a referral to ICE, which may in turn issue a detainer.[10]

Reliance on out-of-school suspensions, expulsions, and school police, coupled with implicit bias, pushes students into the school-to-prison pipeline and puts them and their families at increased risk for transgenerational negative outcomes. These punitive policies have no place in our schools. Though zero tolerance policies are decreasing as a result of activism, research, and pressure to implement alternatives, racial disparities are narrowing at a slower rate. For instance, after a statewide "Fix School Discipline" campaign in California, out-of-school suspensions declined by more than 30 percent for all students. Black students, however, continued to be suspended at roughly four times the rate of whites, about the same as before the campaign.[11]

Restorative Justice in Schools

The communitarian values and belief in the equal dignity of all human beings that are inherent to restorative justice offer hope, resonating strongly with the African American tradition of education for liberation. The first documented use of restorative justice in schools was in 1994, when it was used as a response to an assault at a high school in Queensland, Australia. Positive outcomes of pilot studies led to expansion in more than one hundred schools, after which restorative justice practices in schools were adopted widely across Australia and around the globe.[12] It has become increasingly popular in the United States as evidence mounts showing that it successfully reduces suspensions and expulsions and decreases racial disparities.[13] Further, Department of Justice and Department of Education school discipline directives during the Obama era warned that racial discrimination was not just something limited to the 1960s; it continues in our schools. These directives also mandated districts to transform exclusionary discipline policies or else face federal civil rights lawsuits.

There are growing numbers of studies establishing the effectiveness of school-based restorative justice in reducing suspensions, expulsions, and police referrals, while improving academic outcomes and decreasing violence.[14] For instance, according to a 2015 implementation study of whole-school restorative justice in Oakland that compared schools with restorative justice to schools without, from 2011 to 2014, graduation rates in restorative schools increased by 60 percent compared to a 7 percent increase in nonrestorative schools; reading scores increased 128 percent versus 11 percent; and the dropout rate decreased 56 percent versus 17 percent. Harm was repaired in 76 percent of conflict circles, with students learning to talk instead of fight through differences at home and at school, and more than 88 percent of teachers said that restorative practices were very or somewhat helpful in managing difficult student behaviors.[15]

Even without the research gold standard of double-blind randomized controlled trials, school-based restorative justice is considered a promising practice, with virtually all states in the nation having adopted it in some form. Very few studies, however, focus on the potential of restorative justice to reduce racial disparities in school discipline.[16] Oakland, California, and Denver, Colorado, are leading the way.

Restorative Justice for Oakland Youth (RJOY; Oakland, CA)

Restorative Justice for Oakland Youth (RJOY), a national thought leader in practicing restorative justice in ways that emphasize its intersections with racial justice and honor its indigenous ethos, launched California's first urban school-based restorative justice pilot at an Oakland middle school in 2006. The pilot used restorative conversations and circles proactively to create a culture of connectivity and responsively provide an alternative to exclusionary school discipline. Suspension rates plummeted by 87 percent during the first two years, violence and teacher attrition were eradicated, and academic outcomes increased.[17] By 2010, with youth organizing and RJOY's advocacy and assistance, the Oakland Unified School District (OUSD) adopted restorative justice as official policy and committed significant staff and financial resources to fund these efforts.

Now, nearly forty OUSD restorative schools implement a wide range of restorative practices that both proactively strengthen community and responsively repair harm. These practices include restorative conversations, conferencing and circles, mediation, and a strong student-led component. Restorative practices are also often co-implemented with other school climate strategies such as Positive Behavioral

50

Intervention Systems and initiatives coming out of the Offices of Equity and African American Male Achievement. From 2012 to 2017, overall suspension rates in OUSD dropped by nearly 55 percent, from 7.4 percent to 3.3 percent. Though disparities remain, the black/white discipline gap narrowed from 12.1 percent to 6.4 percent, or a 47 percent decrease. The Latino/white gap narrowed from 3.4 percent to 1.4 percent, a 59 percent gap reduction.[18]

Notably, an important motivation to adopt restorative justice district-wide as official policy, as stated in the 2010 school board resolution, was the legal imperative to address racial disparity in school discipline. The US Department of Education launched an investigation against the Oakland school district for civil rights violations in school discipline; and, as part of the settlement agreement, the district agreed, among other things, to use restorative justice to reduce the disparate rate of arresting, suspending, and expelling black students compared to their white counterparts.

Padres & Jóvenes Unidos/Denver Public Schools (Denver, CO)

In 1992, parents conducted a yearlong protest of a Denver grade school where mischievous Spanish-speaking kids were forced to sit on the floor in a corner at lunch, while mischievous English-speaking kids sat at a special table. The parents requested an apology for the discrimination, and though they never received it, the principal was eventually fired. This parent protest marked the beginning of a group that in 2000 came to be known as Padres & Jóvenes Unidos. By 2006, the group spurred a collaboration

51

with Denver Public Schools (DPS) and the teachers' union to launch a restorative justice pilot program at four schools to address racial disparities in disciplinary practices. The success of the pilot, coupled with continued organizing, led DPS administrators in 2009 to adopt restorative justice as official school discipline policy and expand restorative justice practices to additional schools. With this expansion, DPS shifted restorative justice from an isolated program in individual schools to a district-wide philosophical and values-based approach and practice. Between 2006 and 2013, the DPS overall suspension rate dropped from 10.58 percent to 5.63 percent, a decline of nearly 47 percent. The suspension rate for African Americans fell 7 percent and for Latinos, approximately 6 percent. Though the discipline gap between African Americans and their white counterparts persists, the gap narrowed from a twelve-point gap in 2006 to just over an eight-point gap in 2013, a reduction of 33 percent.[19] In 2016, Padres & Jóvenes Unidos gave DPS an overall grade of C+ for its efforts to improve the disciplinary process and end the school-to-prison pipeline. Their Community Accountability Report Card shows DPS is making progress, but not enough, in eliminating racial disparities in school discipline.

Tips for Reducing Racial Disparities in School Discipline

The following vignette offers insight into suggestions for ways to reduce school discipline racial disparities.

An Oakland-based restorative justice consultant attended a meeting of school administrators in a nearby large school district located in a mostly upscale white county with pockets of high-poverty schools in communities of color. Historically, these schools had high levels of exclusionary discipline coupled with large racial disparities. Three administrators, tasked with drafting plans to address these issues, read their plans aloud. Whether proposing interventions such as mental health services, peer mediation, character development, or conflict-resolution programs, each plan focused on student behavioral deficits. Colleagues gave positive feedback, but the restorative justice consultant remained silent. When asked his opinion, he responded with a question: "Who makes the decisions that result in high levels of racially disproportionate suspensions, expulsions, and arrests?" After a long silence, one administrator finally admitted, "We do." Nodding, the consultant then asked, "And what systemic factors are involved?" "Punitive discipline policy, school segregation, school financing, and teaching quality are some." He replied that while the proposals to alter student behavior might help, little will change without additional interventions addressing implicit bias and student-teacher relationships as well as district efforts to alter policies and the larger institutional context that maintains racialized hierarchies.

I offer three specific strategies to implement restorative justice in schools in a way that will reduce racial disparities.

1. Simultaneously Address Relationships, Institutional Racism, and Implicit Bias

Too often we locate responsibility for school discipline issues and racial disparities in the children and their perceived cognitive or developmental deficits, stopping there, as did the school administrators in the vignette above. This is not surprising—we are socialized to view the world through a lens that centers on the individual. Though this behavioral and psychological approach may be well-meaning, it is shortsighted. Strategies to create equal educational opportunity in our schools require much more, including rigorous and ongoing professional development for all staff in restorative justice. There is some evidence that teachers who implement restorative justice with high fidelity will be perceived as more respectful of students of all racial groups, will have more positive relationships with all students, and will therefore be less likely to rely on punitive school discipline approaches than low-restorative-justice-implementing practitioners.[20] The inference is that implicit bias will be reduced if teacher-student classroom relationships are of better quality. Relational strategies that are race-neutral, however, are not likely to reduce school discipline disparities. Holistic relational strategies that simultaneously interrogate the bias and systemic factors that historically maintain racial hierarchies in education will likely be more productive.[21]

Two restorative justice practitioners with a consulting firm in Northern California decided that, based on the ubiquitous, insidious, and harmful nature of bias in our culture, they would not offer restorative justice trainings to cities, districts, and schools without first requiring them to undergo an equity training, at least three hours in duration. The restorative justice training that follows then weaves in and applies what has been learned from the equity training. This proved to be a tough decision to live with; school administrators and potential clients question why they and their schools need it, vehemently insisting on the restorative justice training only. But the firm remains resolute.

Restorative justice trainers working in schools—and in other applications—would do well to adopt a similar stance. All adults at a school site, including those in the chain of decision making that leads to racially disparate outcomes, do not only need quality restorative justice training, coaching, and mentoring. They also need rigorous and continuing equity training to develop a more nuanced awareness of structural and institutional racism, learn how they personally reproduce structural inequalities through individual bias, and explore strategies to unlearn it. In other words, we need adults at schools and throughout districts to be high implementers of *both* restorative justice *and* racial justice.

Confronting one's own bias is a fraught subject, and it is important that the design and facilitation of implicit bias trainings address the tendency of white educators to feel they stand accused of racism, triggering defensiveness and shutdown. Effective trainings allow participants to be open about acknowledging, exploring, and ultimately unlearning their own bias. White restorative justice practitioners in Oakland and elsewhere are designing whiteness trainings using restorative justice principles to create affinity spaces where persons can unearth and explore their own biases amongst themselves with trained facilitators. In restorative affinity spaces, white participants are less likely to feel shamed and humiliated, and the burden to teach or comfort does not fall upon people of color.

Ricardo Martinez, codirector of Denver-based Padres & Jóvenes Unidos, said words to the effect that we need to press not so much for changes in student behavior, but for changes in adult behaviors. The point is well-taken: it is misguided to propose only youth-focused strategies to rectify racial disparities; we also need interventions that focus on adult behaviors, especially those influenced by implicit bias. I would add we also need interventions that transform systems and policies that perpetuate racialized hierarchies in educational institutions.

2. Develop District-Community Collaborations

Systems interventions create the opportunity for educators and school-based restorative justice practitioners to collaborate with community-based groups, like Padres & Jóvenes Unidos and Restorative Justice for Oakland Youth. These collaborations not only enrich classroom curricula about culture and history and launch restorative justice pilot programs, but also press for public policy changes in support of a racial justice–conscious restorative justice and related strategies. Systems interventions might also involve allying with youth and community activists to press for local, state, and federal legislation to transform segregated schools, inequitable teacher quality, and school financing patterns, as well as to fund equity and restorative justice training, coaching, and implementation.

3. Develop District-University Partnerships

Another effective strategy to transform zero tolerance and interrupt the racialized school-to-prison pipeline is to enter into partnerships with area universities to develop and monitor data and conduct rigorous research on school discipline and racial disparities. A good example is the researcher-practitioner partnership between the University of Denver Graduate School of Social Work and the Office of Social-Emotional Learning at Denver Public Schools. The partners work closely together, regularly meeting over the course of the school year both to track race-related school discipline data as well as develop specific trainings, coaching, and relational interventions to reduce exclusionary discipline and narrow racial disparities. They also monitor the impact of these interventions, continually modifying them to improve efficacy. Additional goals of the partnership are to use research to inform local policy, programs, and practices and to work with policy makers and practitioners to identify and implement effective prevention and intervention strategies.

Conclusion

Being a warrior and healer in the context of school-based restorative justice practice means practicing with heightened and active awareness of our own bias, implicit or explicit, and of systemic factors in our schools that perpetuate harm. A few of the many such factors include financing disparities for schools in communities of color, tracking and special education placements, the school-to-prison pipeline, and racial disparities in discipline. It also means creating school cultures of care, connectivity, and healing.

5.
Restorative Justice and Transforming Mass Incarceration

MPATAPO

The knot of reconciliation symbolizes peacemaking after strife. After conflict we have made peace and are bound together in harmonious reconciliation.

From virtually its inception, the US justice system has been used to brutally subjugate black people and expropriate their labor power. This chapter exposes the hideous and mostly hidden genealogy of the US justice system in white supremacy. It also confronts the afterlife of slavery in mass incarceration and looks at how both restorative justice practitioners and prison activists are responding to it, including in ways that are complementary with one another. The chapter urges activists to continue to seek radical systems change and abolition while experimenting with non-carceral ways of responding to community harm. It further invites restorative justice practitioners to develop a praxis of repairing relational damage that is nurtured by an active vision of radically transforming the justice system and its inherited and inherent racial inequities.

Roots of the US Punishment System

Incarceration as a form of punishment in the United States arose in 1790, when Philadelphia's Walnut Street Jail was converted from a pretrial detention facility to a state penitentiary. Until this time, accused persons were jailed solely to await trial and sentencing. Instead of incarceration, the sentence later imposed involved public and corporal punishment like stocks, whippings, burnings, or being buried alive. Ironically, given this historical context, the penitentiary emerged as a humane, Enlightenment-era reform. Theoretically, the confined person could, in the solitude of their cell, pray, confess, seek penitence, and find redemption. The Walnut Street Jail's early experiment with this penal practice prompted the construction of Eastern State Pennsylvania's Penitentiary, opening in 1829, where the solitary system was implemented on a large scale. Eastern State's radial and panopticon-like floor plan and system of solitary confinement became the model for prisons worldwide.[1]

Though initially a reform to humanize punishment, the purpose of the prison transformed after the Civil War, when states commandeered it to capture the bodies and labor of the newly freed slaves. Before the war, when enslaved persons endured torturous punishment by their owners, 99 percent of prisoners were white. This flipped after emancipation.

In 1865, the Thirteenth Amendment made slavery unlawful, except to punish convicts. Slavery had dominated the Southern economy. Emancipation decimated it. Consequently, Southern legislatures, as well as some in the North, seized on the Amendment's loophole by enacting Black Codes, essentially a reincarnation of Slave Codes that criminalized blackness and usurped the justice system to push Africans back into neo-slavery through the practice of convict leasing. Black Codes made it a crime for blacks to walk beside a railroad, spit, drink, speak loudly, or make insulting gestures before a white man. Absence from work or inability to prove you worked branded you a criminal. A vagrancy fine you had no resources to pay could land you in convict labor camps. Black Codes generated a steady stream of bodies that the state leased out to industrialists and agriculturalists, producing enormous revenues, both public and private. Every cotton harvest season saw a surge of arrests in cotton-growing counties. Surges also occurred in the run-up to recruitment visits by mining or lumber agents. Tens of thousands were arrested in these sweeps. Many were kidnapped or jailed for petty offenses so soon after passage of the Thirteenth Amendment that they never knew freedom.

From county courthouses and jails, men were leased to local plantations, lumber camps, factories, and railroads. Black prisoners found themselves toiling on old slave plantations, sometimes even working for their former slave masters. The lash, shackles, chains, and overseers, emblems of slavery, became the prison's tools of choice. However, convict leasing was worse than slavery, unimaginably, given what enslaved persons endured.[2]

Foreshadowing today's heartrending criminalization of black children, one-third of the inmates in labor camps were adolescent boys. Black family members daily lived in terror of being disappeared, brutalized, and separated from their loved ones. Though a small percentage of all convict laborers, women were not spared; thousands were ensnared, vulnerable to racial and sexual assault. In the labor camps, overseers often drowned newborn babies in the river solely to unencumber their mothers' labor power. Forced into backbreaking labor, starved, beaten, tortured, sexually violated, chained, and forced to live in squalor, black people suffered from disease and died by the thousands, with the death toll at some camps approaching 50 percent.[3]

Under chattel slavery, where enslaved Africans were personal property, slaveholders had an incentive to protect their investment—after all, slaves were expensive to purchase. But under convict leasing, profiteering postbellum industrialists and agriculturalists, who were responsible for the housing, feeding, and care of black prisoners, had no such incentive and thus spent virtually nothing on upkeep. Black labor was cheap and fungible, and when one laborer died, the employer needed only lease another.

Near the turn of the century, the National Association for the Advancement of Colored People (NAACP), the International Labor Defense (ILD) Committee, and other activists and journalists publicized dramatic stories of the abuse and wretched conditions of convict laborers through lawsuits and newspaper accounts. These exposés turned public opinion against convict leasing, forcing Southern states gradually to abolish it.

Chain Gangs and Peonage

Though outlawed by every state by the 1930s, convict leasing was replaced by the no less terrifying chain gangs, or peonage. Chain gangs were originally adopted in the colonies to transport, control, and terrorize African slaves. Prison authorities utilized the chain gang after the Civil War and fall of Reconstruction, to re-enslave free blacks, forcing them under the overseer's whip to do the backbreaking labor of pounding rock, shoveling dirt, and clearing terrain to create roads and build up the infrastructure of the South. The vast majority of prisoners in the chain gangs were black men, and law enforcement manipulated the law to ensnare black people into the chain gang camps. They were chained and shackled together in groups, day and night, and forced to work, eat, and sleep together. The chains and shackles exposed prisoners to painful ulcers and dangerous infections. Thousands lost their lives to abuse and malnutrition.

Postbellum blacks were also captured and forced into labor through debt slavery, or peonage, also made possible by the loophole in the Thirteenth Amendment. Typically, through manipulation, the criminal justice system found black people guilty of Black Code–type violations and fined them. When they were unable to pay, an agriculturalist or industrialist stepped in to cover the fines, and the convicted person was forced to work without pay until the debt was discharged. Black people were also forced into peonage through sharecropping, where former slave plantation owners allowed blacks to use their land in return for a share of the crops produced on their portion of land. Manipulations of chain gangs, peonage, and sharecropping—along with the use of chains, guards, dogs, and terror—trapped black laborers in a continuous work-without-pay cycle.

Abolition of Debt Slavery

In 1940, activists and the ILD organized the Abolish Peonage Committee and, with the help of the NAACP and lawyers including Thurgood Marshall, pressed the Justice Department to take legal action to stop peonage. Finally, in 1941, President Franklin Roosevelt took executive action to abolish it, recognizing these barbarous human rights violations could undermine the war effort by giving the Nazis a propaganda boon. This abominable, yet concealed, chapter of US history finally came to a close.[4]

These ubiquitous forms of postbellum neo-slavery, however, firmly established the nation's enduring practice of using the justice system as an instrument to brutally subordinate black people. It also established the nation's lasting practice of equating blackness with criminality. Reverberations of the postbellum criminalization of black life remain visible in today's extrajudicial killings of black people and in incessant reports of whites calling police on "suspicious" black people, whether it be two black men awaiting the arrival of their business partner in Starbucks or a black female Yale graduate student asleep in a common area.

The Neo-Slavery of Mass Incarceration

The terrors of slavery and convict leasing survived with debt slavery, the chain gang, and then lynching. They also lived on through Jim Crow, laws that enforced inequality and strict segregation of the races in the Southern states from the end of Reconstruction

63

until 1965. Even after each of these was denounced,[5] the violence at their core has continued to live on with mass incarceration.

Incarcerating at a rate without equal in the world, the United States comprises about 5 percent of the world's population yet almost 25 percent of its prison population. In 2016, there were 2.2 million people in the nation's prisons and jails—a 500 percent increase over forty years, with a total of 6.7 million people under correctional supervision.[6] Policy changes, not crime increases, fueled expansion. Nixon's War on Drugs and Crime in the early 1970s intentionally engendered mass incarceration to suppress the 1960s black freedom movement,[7] not unlike the terror of the late 1870s that routed Reconstruction. Additional drivers of mass incarceration include mandatory sentencing laws, deindustrialization and resulting joblessness, and the emergence of private prisons, the correctional lobby, and unfettered prosecutorial power.

The US criminal justice system's historical roots in slavery and its progeny are visible today in the hugely disproportionate numbers of people of color who are incarcerated. Black and brown people are 60 percent of US prisoners, yet only 20 percent of the general population. Blacks are six times more likely to be incarcerated than whites. One in four black men is or has been incarcerated.[8] Though their wrongdoing levels are comparable, black boys are incarcerated at rates twenty to twenty-four times higher than white boys in some states.[9] Black and white Americans sell and use drugs at similar rates, but blacks are nearly three times as likely to be arrested and serve significantly longer sentences.[10]

Incarceration has grave consequences. Imprisonment for one year takes two years off one's life span[11] and reduces annual wages by 40 percent.[12] More than six million currently or formerly incarcerated persons are legally discriminated against in employment, housing, access to education, and public benefits and disenfranchised or denied the right to vote, as well. With the period of disenfranchisement ranging from permanent loss to restoration following the completion of one's sentence,[13] Blacks are disenfranchised at a rate greater than four times that of their nonblack counterparts.

Girls and women of color are the fastest-growing segments of the incarcerated population. Black women, who make up 13 percent of the US female population, represent 30 percent of incarcerated women. Most have suffered physical or sexual assault at the hands of the state or their men, and a majority in state prisons are mothers of minor children.[14] Akin to slavery, most devastating is the impact mass incarceration has on families. Black children are six times as likely as their white counterparts to have or have had an incarcerated parent, and one in four black children has a currently or formerly incarcerated parent. Children with incarcerated parents perform worse across a range of educational, health, and social measures than children without incarcerated parents. They are more likely to develop learning disabilities, have lower GPAs, and be pushed out of school. They are also more likely to experience homelessness, depression, anxiety and PTSD, and chronic disease as adults, compared to those whose parents are not incarcerated. Parental incarceration exacerbates family poverty, and growing up poor creates toxic stress and elevated cortisol, which disrupts activity in areas of the brain

65

responsible for emotional regulation and anxiety. Children of the incarcerated are thus more likely to engage in trauma-driven misconduct, which results in increased likelihood of being suspended, expelled, or arrested at school and pushed into the school-to-prison pipeline. Because youth incarceration is the strongest predictor of adult incarceration, children find themselves trapped in a self-perpetuating transgenerational dynamic of cascading negative health, economic, and education outcomes.[15]

Prison Activism and Abolitionism

Over the last two decades, activists have resisted the surge of racialized mass incarceration and its appalling impacts, with abolitionists leading the way. The abolition movement is a loose national network of individuals and groups who locate the origins of the prison in slavery and act to abolish its use because of that historical context. Abolitionists point out that the nation has decided that slavery, convict leasing, and debt slavery have no place; we have abolished them. They then argue that, because prisons are a direct descendant of these institutions, the prison too should be rendered obsolete.

Abolitionists, representing a continuum of resistance starting with nineteenth-century slavery abolition, deliver a radical critique of racial capitalism. Racial capitalism refers to a socioeconomic order in which all social institutions are inextricably bound up with the slave trade and slavery, indigenous land seizure, genocide, and colonization. Drawing on the scholarship of iconic public intellectual W.E.B. Du Bois, Harvard Professor of African and African American Studies Walter Johnson argues:

There was no such thing as capitalism without slavery; the history of Manchester never happened without the history of Mississippi. The history of capitalism, it must be emphasized, is a history of wages as well as whips, of factories as well as plantations, of whiteness as well as blackness, of "freedom" as well as slavery.[16]

Today, racial capitalism uses prisons to manage marginalized populations, especially people of color. Neoliberal policies in the last decades have shifted massive amounts of wealth from working- and middle-class families to the wealthiest 1 percent through tax cuts, deregulation, and cutting social programs. These policies shred social safety nets[17] and render millions of people unemployed, poor, unhealthy, and homeless, creating "surplus populations." Incarceration is then deployed to contain and manage these populations and the problems created by racial capitalism's failure to address social ills.

Additionally, incarceration continues to be used today—as it was previously during convict leasing, debt slavery, and the chain gangs—to steal the labor of prisoners. Prisoners are routinely used as a source of cheap, nearly free labor. For instance, as we go to press, thousands of prisoners are being used to fight wildfires raging in California. For performing this service of incalculable value for which they risk their lives, they are paid $1 per hour.

Outraged by these conditions, prison activists have been successfully organizing to stop the construction of new prisons and close old ones. For instance, Justice for D.C. Youth convinced the city council to close a juvenile facility in 2009. The No New San

Francisco Jail Coalition stopped the construction of a new jail, while Seattle activists persuaded the city council to declare its intent to end youth incarceration in 2015. In the last decade, fifteen states have closed prisons and twenty-six have decreased the number of people they imprison.[18] The US incarceration rate fell in 2016 to its lowest level in twenty years. Abolitionists and prison activists also work to end discrimination against the formerly incarcerated, including advocating for Ban the Box legislation, which requires employers to remove from hiring applications the check box asking if applicants have a criminal record. Additionally, twenty-nine states have adopted legislation that cuts back on the severity of mandatory-sentencing policies.[19]

Importantly, prison activism has also scored narrative change. A 2017 ACLU poll shows 71 percent of Americans believe incarceration is often counterproductive to public safety,[20] and in 2015, 130 police commissioners and prosecutors called for an end to mass incarceration.[21] Lowered incarceration rates, prison closures, legislative gains, and narrative change are all, in my view, the fruit of three decades of prison activism and abolitionism, not unlike the manner in which broad social advancements were won in the wake of the 1960s civil rights movement.

Complementing these political victories, prison activists and abolitionists, particularly the younger generations, are beginning to go beyond the negative abolitionism of tearing down prisons. They are extending their view to envision and engender a new non-carceral justice. Mariame Kaba's work in Chicago is an example. Standing at the intersection of abolitionism, Black Lives Matter, and restorative and transformative justice, Kaba facilitates community accountability processes in racial justice organizations, often to transform sexual harm. Equally important as dismantling the institution of prison, she asserts, is dismantling the punitive and carceral ways we often respond to harm in our own lives. The very systems we work to dismantle live both outside and inside of us. In developing nonpunitive ways of responding to community harm, Kaba's work prefigures a new justice and set of social relations that do not rely on the carceral state. Kaba explains:

> Abolitionist leader Ruthie Gilmore says abolitionism is equally about presence as absence. The idea of absence pertains to absenting the prison industrial complex. The idea of presence means being present as someone people can turn to when harm occurs so that it is not necessary to turn to the state. Both are abolitionist projects.[22]

Restorative Justice and Mass Incarceration

The restorative justice movement, offering more than just a social services–type intervention, has the potential to engender a new justice that transforms both social relations and social structures. Three restorative justice conferencing programs exemplify this vision of a restorative justice that repairs individual and social harm[23] and interrupts overincarceration of youth of color, thus mitigating a host of long-term negative impacts.

Baltimore's Restorative Responses was the first restorative justice program expressly designed to divert youth of color facing felony charges from incarceration. Restorative Responses offers restorative conferencing for youth in the justice system, in schools, and in communities, an expansive approach that allows for holistic, upstream interventions to protect children from incarceration. Evaluation finds that program graduates reoffend 60 percent less than those going through the justice system.

The express goal of Restorative Community Conferencing, a program of Oakland-based Community Works West (CWW), is to reduce disproportionate incarceration rates of African American and Latinx young people. CWW gets the case before the prosecutor files charges, and youth who comply with their plan completely bypass the justice system, leaving no record of system involvement. Restorative Community Conferencing diverts about one hundred youths per year from incarceration.

Common Justice, based in Brooklyn and the Bronx, offers the first victim services and alternative to incarceration program for young adults with violent felonies. Shattering the stereotype that victims are white and perpetrators are black, Common Justice prioritizes victim services for youth of color, who are statistically at greatest risk of being criminally harmed, yet who are least likely to receive victim services. Additionally, young people responsible for harm who successfully complete their restorative process and plan serve neither jail nor prison time. By attending to the needs and obligations of both victims and offenders, Common Justice diminishes both the impacts of incarceration and the traumatic social costs of discriminatory denial of victim services to youth of color. Common Justice seeks healing equity for all, driven by change in our culture's devaluation of the pain experienced by young men and communities.

While programs seeking to end youth incarceration are of inestimable value, true systems change also requires a parallel organizing strategy to institutionalize restorative justice and other non-carceral community-based healing approaches within justice systems. This strategy would produce both relational and systems change, enhancing the anti-racist impacts and transformative power of the work of both restorative justice practitioners and prison activists. Without these enhanced efforts, restorative justice practitioners address symptoms, not causes, and the prison-industrial complex remains intact. Additionally, we put ourselves in the ethically dubious position of deeming some youth deserving of diversion and others not. RJOY's "restorganizing" to institutionalize restorative justice in schools is an example of this parallel strategy. After three years of advocacy, youth organizing, and implementation of whole-school restorative justice in a pilot program, the school district adopted restorative justice as official school discipline and school culture policy, complete with funding to hire employees to support this new approach.

Integrating Activism and Restorative Justice

The warrior and healer come together in the dual strategy above that provides restorative diversion while promoting systems change. They join in restorganizing. For prison activists, an exclusive focus on changing systems will be counterproductive. No amount of political victories alone will affect the intrapersonal and interpersonal transformations needed. We need healing strategies, not just political ones. At the same time, racial harms are so historicized, structuralized, and normalized that we simply cannot do meaningful healing work if we remain sequestered within interpersonal dimensions. Healing ourselves and our relationships is essential, but it is not sufficient.

Let us also transform histories and systems that have been created precisely to perpetuate harm. Eradicating systemic racism requires a perspective that is systemic and steeped in knowledge of the genealogy of the criminal justice system in white supremacy. Exposing and confronting these painful truths and taking personal responsibility for them require the radical analysis and courage of the warrior.

Kaba reminds us that we must also do the painstaking and emotionally challenging work of transforming ourselves and our relationships, so that we do not replicate the racist and retributive practices of the very institutions we seek to change or abolish. This personal and relational transformation requires the restorative and trauma-informed approach and empathy of the healer. Restorative justice and racial/social justice organizations can join forces to achieve the dual goals of interpersonal healing and systems change.

6.
Toward a Racial Reckoning: Imagining a Truth Process for Police Violence

SESA WORUBAN

Behold the bright sun of transformation and a new beginning.

Maya Angelou proclaimed that "[h]istory, despite its wrenching pain, cannot be unlived, but if faced with courage, need not be lived again."[1] While the nation abolished slavery, the racial terror at its essence continues to haunt us. We are caught in history's pain, living it again and again. Until we engage in a collective process to face and transform this pain, we will perpetually reenact it.

A crucial manifestation of racial terror today is lethal police violence against African Americans. Multiple parties have called for a national truth and reconciliation commission (TRC) to confront and end this epidemic.[2] Some suggest following the South Africa TRC model, but very few have considered whether this strategy would be effective in the US context, and, if so, what it might look like. Applying restorative justice principles and synthesizing lessons from combined TRC models, this chapter posits the requisite elements of a truth process to address police violence against African Americans.

Police Violence

Throughout history, police have served as highly visible enforcers of white supremacy who brutally subjugate black communities. We see this in the paddyrollers' capture of escaped slaves, in convict leasing and debt-slavery-era arrests, in police-assisted lynchings during Reconstruction and the Jim Crow and civil rights period, and, finally, in today's criminalization of blackness and countless killings of black people. Throughout this history, police have been active members of racial terror organizations, have delivered black victims to white mobs, and have failed to protect people of color from racial terror.[3] Recent research finds that black teens are twenty-one times more likely to be killed by police than white teens.

The wave of internationally publicized police killings in the United States during 2014 and 2015 engendered the historic, youth-driven Black Lives Matter movement and sparked an unprecedented national race conversation and public outcry to end police violence against unarmed black people—Michael Brown (Ferguson), Eric Garner (Staten Island), John Crawford III (Dayton), Tamir Rice (Cleveland), Tony Terrell Robinson (Madison), Walter Scott (North Charleston), Freddie Gray (Baltimore), Tenisha Anderson (Cleveland), Sandra Bland (Waller County, Texas), Samuel DuBose (Cincinnati), and countless others since. In the wake of each killing, the nation expresses shock, furor, and an enormous outpouring of grief. Invariably, there is also the cry to bring the responsible officers to justice through criminal prosecution. We pin our hopes on the criminal justice system, knowing that the system rarely indicts police officers and even more rarely convicts them. Further, even successful prosecutions focused on individuals will not stop the pandemic because the problem is systemic. Our justice system itself, intensively punitive and racialized, is a perpetrator of massive harm. This leaves families who have lost loved ones to police violence heartlessly revictimized. If the justice system as we know it cannot adequately address the epidemic of police killings, is there a justice that can? I believe truth processes are our best hope.

The Truth and Reconciliation[4] Model

The earliest truth commissions in the mid-1970s were fact-finding, nonjudicial bodies that sought to unearth buried truths about massive human rights violations, past and ongoing, particularly in Africa and Latin America. Four TRCs stand out as helpful models in designing US truth processes: the South Africa, Canada, Greensboro, and Maine-Wabanaki Commissions.

South Africa's Truth and Reconciliation Commission (SATRC)

The widely renowned and oft-replicated 1994 South African Truth and Reconciliation Commission (SATRC) was formed by the new South African government after it initiated a broad public dialogue about the best way forward after apartheid; it highlighted the need both to unsilence truths and promote reconciliation. The commission was mandated to investigate human rights abuses from 1960 to 1994 and create public spaces where apartheid victims' voices were elevated, heard, and validated. They also recommended reparations for apartheid's victims and heard amnesty petitions for its perpetrators. The SATRC's experiments were a first and have proved historic.

The SATRC also had its shortcomings. The process favored an individualized approach that centered on specific victims and perpetrators (who were applying for amnesty) and their interpersonal reconciliation, giving less attention to the role of apartheid governance structures. The government failed to meaningfully implement reparations. The process falsely equated the abuses committed by the freedom movement with those inflicted by the apartheid regime. Victims publicly recounting and reliving their trauma received inadequate support. Criticisms notwithstanding, the SATRC was internationally hailed for fostering a spirit of forgiveness that allowed the country to make a relatively peaceful transition from apartheid.

Though there is much to learn from the innovations of South Africa's TRC, holding it up as *the* model to implement in the United States overstates the case

76

and elides important differences between the US and South African contexts. In addition to concerns with the limitations above, the SATRC was a top-down, government-initiated process, and South Africa was a nation in transition to Western democracy from apartheid. The above suggest that the SATRC is not the best model for the United States. Perhaps TRCs closer to home offer further insight.

Canada's Truth and Reconciliation Commission

Canada's 2008 Truth and Reconciliation Commission (CTRC) was the first government-sanctioned commission impaneled in a nation not undergoing political transition. Like the SATRC, it was created through a top-down process as part of a CAN$2 billion settlement in a class action to redress massive human rights abuses against aboriginal children. Over a period of one hundred years, aboriginal children were forcibly removed from their homes and placed in Indian Residential Schools, where they were punished for honoring their language and traditions and subjected to unrelenting physical, emotional, and sexual abuse. Though originating from litigation, the commission deployed ground-up strategies, such as traveling to three hundred communities to take evidence from 6,500 witnesses, creating an indigenous elders' advisory council for guidance, and partnering with an indigenous-led NGO. Going beyond interpersonal harm, the CTRC's final report recommended systemic change to redress anti-Aboriginal bias and disparities in Canadian child welfare and other institutions. Prime Minister Stephen Harper also made a formal apology.

Greensboro Truth and Reconciliation Commission

Even closer to home was North Carolina's 2004 Greensboro Truth and Reconciliation Commission (GRTC). The first US commission, it was formed in response to 1979 events when Ku Klux Klansmen and Nazis fired on protesters with police complicity, killing five and injuring ten. A series of all-white juries exonerated police with one minor exception.[5] Two decades after the massacre and failed prosecutions, the Greensboro community remained divided. Though city officials refused to sanction the process, community members formed a grassroots commission that united survivors, police, and former Klansmen and Nazis to give public testimony. The final report called for community healing by way of institutional reform, official apologies, anti-racism police training, public memorials and museum exhibits, and the creation of a community justice center and police review board. The city rejected these recommendations, demonstrating that grassroots-initiated TRCs need the participation of policy makers with the will to implement institutional reform.[6]

Maine-Wabanaki Truth and Reconciliation Commission

Perhaps shedding the brightest light on possibilities for a US truth and reconciliation commission is the Maine-Wabanaki Truth and Reconciliation Commission (MWTRC), the first involving indigenous nations and a state government. In 2012, five Wabanaki tribal chiefs and Maine's governor signed on to the MWTRC to redress human rights abuses stemming from the state child welfare system's forced assimilation of indigenous children. The MWTRC subjected Maine's child-welfare system to scrutiny, addressing both systemic and interpersonal harm.

Though originating from grassroots community organizing, the MWTRC also involved collaboration with government actors. Wabanaki REACH, the commission's community partner, conceptualized and established the MWTRC and played an instrumental role in its realization. They connected the MWTRC to communities and people wishing to testify. They led ceremonies and supported community trauma healing. The MWTRC also provided education on the history of relations between indigenous and nonindigenous peoples and advised the TRC on native child welfare.

The final report recommended a host of systemic reforms, including reform in the state child welfare system, tribal courts, and native foster care services. The commission also recommended the reformation and expansion of sovereignty and the equalization and decolonization of tribal government and state government relations. They proposed changing school curricula to tell the truth about the cultural genocide along with an increase in cultural, training, and educational opportunities.

These four examples demonstrate that, over time and across continents, TRCs have evolved to emphasize reconciliation *and* truth, bottom-up *and* top-down orientations, and systemic *and* interpersonal transformation. They have been applied in established democracies and in countries in transition. At times, they have broadened the national narrative on racial issues by including historically silenced voices. In these ways, they offer guidance on envisioning a US truth process in response to police violence.

Toward a US Truth Process to Address Police Violence

A truth process is an important step on the long and arduous journey to eliminate police killings of African Americans. We need a homegrown model, one informed but not defined by models from another context. No road maps exist, but there are signposts to guide the creation of a US truth process. These signposts consist of the restorative principles of relationality and subsidiarity along with holistic principles.

Relationality

Consistent with the restorative justice principle that we do justice "with" people and not "to" them, it is important that the design of a truth process emerge from an inclusive, participatory planning process that centers on impacted persons. Further, restorative justice is relational, taking the fact of human connection as the starting point for thinking about what justice requires. Freedom is found not in separation from but rather in community with one another. As such, a truth process would not be "simply justice for victims or communities," but justice for all—victims, communities, and wrongdoers.[7]

Subsidiarity

The principle of subsidiarity holds that those directly impacted by an offense should have decision-making powers about their lives; decisions should be made at the lowest levels, rather than by a central authority. Subsidiarity, therefore, requires intentionally creating decentralized, bottom-up, participatory, and radically democratic truth and reconciliation processes. Consonant with a key tenet of critical race theory,[8] these subsidiarity processes should center marginalized voices, elevate counternarratives, and unveil truths that have been historically silenced. Subsidiarity would encourage community ownership[9] of a truth process in the United States to address police violence.

In the United States, I propose a hybrid model akin to that of the Maine-Wabanaki TRC, where a community-based organization with a history of working with survivors of police violence conceptualizes, initiates, and implements the truth process. This organization could form the link to impacted communities and witnesses, provide culturally specific trauma-healing services to witnesses who testify publicly, and facilitate cultural healing circles and ceremonies. Additionally, instead of a single centralized national process, several commissions could operate simultaneously and autonomously in multiple jurisdictions around the country.

These hubs could geographically track and build on the work of police departments already actively engaged in police and community repair and reconciliation efforts. Notably, this includes the work of Chief Lou Dekmar of LaGrange, Georgia, also president of the International Association of Chiefs of Police. In 2017, Dekmar apologized to a local church congregation for the role the city's police department played in the historical LaGrange lynching of sixteen-year-old Austin Calloway, falsely accused of assaulting a white woman, stating:

I sincerely regret and denounce the role our Police Department played in Austin's lynching, both through our action and our inaction. And

81

for that, I'm profoundly sorry. It should never have happened.[10]

Chief Dekmar is one of several law enforcement executives across the nation collaborating with David Kennedy's National Initiative for Building Community Trust and Justice, some or all of whom might participate in the truth process envisioned.[11]

Local hubs would create safe public spaces for youth, families, neighbors, witnesses, and other survivors to share their stories. These spaces would also serve as sites for dialogical encounters between police representatives and families who have lost loved ones to police violence, where harmed persons engage in public truth-telling, and responsible persons take active responsibility to repair wrongdoing. I had the honor of personally witnessing such truth-telling and repair efforts between police chiefs and families who lost loved ones to lynching and police violence at a 2018 gathering co-sponsored by the National Network for Safe Communities and the Civil Rights and Restorative Justice Project. Moved deeply by the dialogue, I imagined this was what it must have felt like during the South Africa truth process. These kinds of dialogical encounters, replicated in five to seven local hubs across the nation, could comprise the truth process infrastructure.

A national resource center could serve the local hubs by networking them and disseminating local discoveries. The center would further provide technical assistance, help to establish training and practice standards, and offer other resources.

As we learned from the Greensboro TRC, successful implementation of recommendations requires the buy-in and participation of government actors. Steps need to be taken, however, to mitigate the risk of co-optation and to ensure political autonomy. This might include declining funding support from the government and assuring that the commission not be comprised of a majority of government actors.

Holistic Approaches

Addressing harm holistically requires attention to recognizing and restoring not only relational, but also structural dimensions of harm. Healthy social relationships *and* social structures are the goals. Indeed, the normalization of white supremacy, enacted through individual, institutional, and structural racism, is so totalizing that any efforts at uprooting it need to be multidimensional and all-encompassing. A US truth process cannot rely on a centralized, hierarchical approach guided by ostensible experts; we have to roll up our sleeves and do this work ourselves on ground levels. This means working holistically and simultaneously on intrapersonal, intragroup, intergroup, and systems levels. Circle processes at most, but not all, levels are well suited for this type of multilevel work.

Intrapersonal work within each hub would build capacity to recognize and interrupt ways in which white people, including police officers, personally perpetuate institutional and structural racism. This might entail developing individual mind-body awareness practices, such as meditation or yoga, to hone the capacity to identify and interrupt internal racist responses in the moment they arise. Individual participants in the hubs could also look to the growing body of work in the field of whiteness for de-biasing strategies, studying alone or in study circles.

83

At the intragroup level, the hubs could engage in collective work related to whiteness, as in the whiteness study circles mentioned above, and internalized oppression involving circles for people of color. Further, police officers and white community members could participate in interactive, participatory implicit bias trainings, ideally conducted in restorative circles. Showing Up for Racial Justice, Coming to the Table, and white restorative justice practitioners in Restorative Justice for Oakland Youth offer excellent training resources for use at this level.

At the intergroup/systems level, hubs could host facilitated encounters, using circles or conferencing processes, that involve law enforcement representatives and families who have lost loved ones to police violence and affected community members to engage in truth-telling; identify harms, needs, and obligations; and collaboratively develop collective-action strategies. This is a circle that operates at the intergroup and systems levels simultaneously. Hubs could also offer intergroup-level circle processes involving community members who are white and others who are persons of color to engage in cross-racial dialogue.

Theater, dance, music, and other arts can play a central role in this holistic approach operating at intergroup levels, particularly art forms that are radically inclusive on the basis of race and other historically marginalized identities (e.g., age, gender, gender expression, formerly incarcerated status). Such art might intentionally bring together two or more polarized communities to engage in dialogue and ultimately to create a new narrative that fosters change on structural levels. The critically acclaimed

Antigone in Ferguson is an example. Bryan Doerries, creator and director, fuses dramatic readings of Sophocles's *Antigone*, an ancient story of death, law enforcement, and civil disobedience resonating with the contemporary story of the police killing of Michael Brown, with live choral music to catalyze powerful and healing postperformance discussions with the audience about race and social justice. Of note, *Antigone in Ferguson*'s diverse choir unites police officers, activists, youth, teachers, and others from Ferguson and elsewhere. The intentionality of bringing diverse and sometimes polarized communities together, both onstage and in the audience, serves to create an inclusive space for those impacted by police violence, including law enforcement representatives, in which to share their stories and engage in transformational dialogue.

Envisioned Outcomes

It is impossible to predict what specific action recommendations would emerge from a truth and reconciliation process in response to police violence. If history is any guide, it could result in:

- Public apologies;
- Reparations and restitution to those harmed;
- Corrections to official historical records;
- Memorials to the fallen, including statues, memorial plaques, headstones, museums, and street renamings;
- Public art, poetry, film, and theater that unearth truths about racial violence; and
- Proposals to demilitarize police and reinvest in community-based solutions.

It might also engender calls to use restorative and other nonpunitive practices to stop violence and interrupt the racialized school-to-prison pipeline and mass incarceration. The process might also call for revised public school textbooks and curricula that tell the truth, from multiple perspectives, about white supremacist police practices and the movements that arose to resist them. Calls could be made for police trainings in restorative and community policing practices or residency requirements for new police hires.[12] Organizations such as Showing Up for Racial Justice and Black Lives Matter offer further possibilities for alliance and action through their efforts in political education and direct actions.

Truth and Reconciliation
Racial and social justice activists tend to emphasize truth-telling, where they create spaces for survivors of police violence to give public testimony about injustice and where they often respond with a demand for punitive justice. Conversely, restorative justice practitioners are more likely to emphasize reconciliation. The envisioned truth and reconciliation process will benefit greatly from the convergence of racial justice activism and restorative justice praxis, with each complementing and completing the other. For an efficacious process, we need to draw on the wisdoms of both.

Conclusion
In the face of the immense and diverse terrain to be covered on the journey toward a more racially reconciled America, no single process will be enough. However, a truth process to address police violence

against African Americans is a crucial first step. It could also serve as a prototype to guide future truth efforts in the United States addressing epidemics such as sexual assault, xenophobia, transphobia, mass incarceration, wealth inequality, and climate catastrophe. The relational, radically democratic, and holistic truth process I envision, based on restorative justice principles and processes, will begin to allow us to face history's pain with courage so it need not be lived again.

7.
A Way Forward

ODO NNYEW FIE KWAN
Love never loses its way home.

Introduction

Even absent an existing formal truth and reconciliation process and without significant numbers of race-conscious restorative justice programs, Americans are, seemingly spontaneously, telling the truth about white supremacy, slavery, lynching, and police violence like never before in history. This phenomenal development signals the time is right for initiatives to face, take responsibility for, and transform painful histories of race.

I began this book by sharing my personal journey to racial and restorative justice, to becoming a warrior and healer. I end by picking up the thread of my life's journey to reflect on how my notion of justice has evolved in tandem with my personal evolution as a warrior-healer. I conclude with an exhortation to restorative justice practitioners and activists to live and work at the intersection of healing and activism.

Facing and Repairing History's Pain

It is encouraging that Americans are now making efforts to confront the pain of our national history. A multitude of unparalleled, albeit siloed, truth-telling, reconciliation, reparations, and memorialization efforts have been bubbling up all across the nation since the rise of the Black Lives Matter movement in 2014. Several examples include:

- The Civil Rights and Restorative Justice Project's work to unearth and seek public apologies and reparations for cold cases that implicate local law enforcement in lynchings and other racial terror in the South during the civil rights era;
- The Equal Justice Initiative's truth-telling and memorialization work through their lynching and slavery reports, historical marker projects, and groundbreaking state-of-the-art slavery and lynching museum openings in 2018;
- The Slave Dwelling Project's work to preserve extant slave dwellings and engage the public in discourse about the dwellings, slave rebellions, Maroon communities, and the underground railroad;
- Establishment of reparations funds in Chicago and Charlottesville.
- White people in ever-increasing numbers (including members of such national organizations as Showing Up for Racial Justice and Coming to the Table) unearthing

family histories of complicity with slavery
and lynching, publishing and teaching about
whiteness, identifying and transforming ways
in which they personally perpetuate structural
and institutional racism, and engaging in racial
healing dialogue and collective anti-racist action;
- The Confederate memorial removal movement
spanning thirty-one cities with 110 memorials
removed as of June 2018;
- The Smithsonian Institution's 2016 opening
of the National Museum of African American
History and Culture with the slavery exhibit as
its centerpiece;
- Ferguson's Truth-Telling Project's and
Fellowship of Reconciliation's truth-telling
and reparations campaign and reparations
symposia, including at Harvard University;
- National truth-telling, public apology,
reconciliation, and memorialization efforts
involving law enforcement and family members
of lynching and police violence victims,
organized by the Civil Rights and Restorative
Justice Project and National Network for Safe
Communities.
- The W.K. Kellogg Foundation's 2016 launch
of a national Truth, Racial Healing &
Transformation enterprise.

Surging public truth-telling about systemic harm
against black people also includes reverberations in
popular culture. Colin Kaepernick-led NFL protests
and Beyoncé's 2016 Panther-inspired Superbowl show
rocked the sports world. On the arts and culture
front, Kendrick Lamar's mass incarceration–themed

2016 Grammy performance, along with TV shows like *Black-ish* and films like *Get Out, BlindSpotting, Sorry to Bother You,* and *BlackkKlansman,* bring conversations about state-sanctioned racial terror into our living rooms.

This truth-telling is accompanied by a similar unprecedented upwelling in universities. Institutions like Harvard University, Georgetown University, Brown University, the University of Virginia, and nearly fifty others participate in the rapidly growing Universities Studying Slavery network, researching and telling the truth about their complicity with slavery and the slave trade and offering apologies, reparations, and memorialization efforts.

Even the language of race is changing. Since the birth of our nation, the term *white supremacy* was always pushed into the margins of mainstream discourse. Now, however, the term is becoming normalized, appearing in scholarly journals, books, social media, and the print and electronic media. This signals that denial about our collective biography is giving way to truth. Similarly, the word *reparations* has been marginalized, and even demonized, at least when it came to the demands of black people. This is shifting now as well, with the sea change in race relations effected by Black Lives Matter and Ta-Nehisi Coates's 2014 *Atlantic* magazine article, "The Case for Reparations."[1]

Suggesting that the soil is prepared to plant the seeds of truth-telling, restorative and racial justice, and healing, these phenomenal developments offer hope against the backdrop of Trump-era bleakness and its characteristic rise of racial hate groups and upsurge of hate violence.

Evolution of My Ideas about Justice

Along the trajectory of my lifelong quest as warrior-healer, my ideas about justice have continually evolved and expanded. Coming of age in the Deep South, justice meant freeing my people from de jure discrimination and the yoke of Jim Crow. When I went to the North and experienced de facto racial discrimination, justice required gaining equality for all my people, north and south. Traveling to California to attend graduate school, I became aware of the oppression of people of color and justice then expanded to encompass liberation for all people of color subjugated by colonialism and neocolonialism. I later learned about gender oppression, and so justice required freedom from systems of heteropatriarchy, as well. Continuing the journey, I became aware of class exploitation, and justice expanded to include emancipation of working people exploited by capitalism. When I traveled to Africa to live with and learn from indigenous healers, I came to understand that the historical imperative of our times is not solely to change the complexion, gender, or class of those in power. If we are to move into a future, we need to do no less than reimagine what it means to be human in relationship to one another and to the Earth and her inhabitants.

Today, I believe there is nothing more subversive than helping to midwife a new evolutionary shift of the human species into an era where we will no longer be entranced with socioeconomic formations and ways of being and thinking that produce disconnection, domination, and devastation. Instead, we can be present upon the Earth in ways that bring healing, wholeness, and a sense of the sacred in our connection with one another and with all of creation. Learning about restorative justice and its indigenous ethos has helped me to integrate all these evolving ideas into an even more capacious justice, one that produces radically inclusive, decentralized, and democratic spaces that offer the possibility of recognizing, taking responsibility for, and repairing harm, both interpersonal and structural. My dream is that restorative justice, as a worldview inspired by indigenous insights and as a medium of holistic change—on intrapersonal, interpersonal, intragroup, intergroup, and systems levels—might help move us from an ethic of separation, domination, and extreme individualism to one of collaboration, partnership, and interrelatedness. In this sense, I would say that this integral vision of restorative justice is potentially more subversive than the visions of any of the social movements in which I have been involved since the 1950s.

The future of restorative justice, social justice, and the entire nation depends on how we remediate racial inequities. We cannot remain true to ourselves as healers of harm if we practice restorative justice in ways that ignore race and turn a blind eye to the ubiquitous, systemic harms that continue today. As warriors for justice, we will never be effective if we do not also work toward—and aspire to personally model—healing approaches. We face challenging questions:

- How can white people become conscious of their own implicit bias and more skillful about interrupting the nuanced ways in which they, whether facilitators or activists, may embody and perpetuate legacies of slavery?

- How do we develop greater skill in identifying and remediating historical harm that plays out in the restorative processes we daily facilitate or in the racial and social justice campaigns where we organize?
- How can we, as both restorative justice practitioners and racial justice activists, be more skillful in designing, implementing, and evaluating restorative justice and restorganizing approaches designed to eradicate racial disparities across social institutions?

The way we address these central questions will determine our effectiveness both as practitioners and activists and, ultimately, the future of both movements.

We US-based practitioners are being called to reimagine the way we understand and practice restorative justice. For white practitioners particularly, this means developing and honing skills to identify and address historical and systemic harm, navigate racial differences, and facilitate restorative justice encounters involving racially diverse participants or involving racial conflict.

Practitioners and activists alike, particularly those who are white, need ongoing trainings and professional development opportunities that include modules on unlearning racism, whiteness, and the history of the US justice system in slavery and white supremacy. Both groups can avail themselves of the expanding extraordinary body of work in the emerging field of critical whiteness studies that examines whiteness in the context of individual, institutional, and structural racism and offers multiple practical anti-racist strategies.[2] Both groups can also avail themselves of the neuroscientific and practical discoveries in the growing field of trauma studies, particularly those of us working in communities and schools of historically traumatized persons.

Let us imagine how a consciousness about the healing of systemic harm committed against members of historically marginalized groups might animate and pervade *all* our restorative work. Let us consider how we might creatively conceive of multiple ways in which every restorative justice process we facilitate or participate in might involve truth-telling and promote healing of historical harm.

Ultimately, I invite us to imagine how—through the deeply transformed relationships arising from reeducation, transracial and restorative dialogue, and mutual collaboration of race-conscious restorative justice practitioners with healing-conscious racial justice practitioners—we will develop the capacity to take sustainable collective action to transform people, institutions, structures, and systems of power. We *can* build a new future together, and we *can* create a nation that is no longer racially fractured.

Challenge yourself to be a healer and activist for justice. Don't feel you have to choose one or the other. Be both. See activism as a form of social healing and interpersonal healing as a form of social justice. Transform and heal yourself as you transform and heal the world. Be the change you wish to see. History is calling us to be warriors and healers, like Rolihlahla Nelson Mandela was; like Grace Lee Boggs was; like Ericka Huggins is; and like the International Indigenous Youth of Standing Rock are. Let us answer history's call.

Healers and warriors are not opposites; they are complementarities. Moving beyond binaries, we need not embrace one and reject the other. We can hold them both as one. A single individual might embody the warrior-healer principle. A collaborative may also give life to this principle—for instance, when restorative justice practitioners and activists engage in restorganizing to end youth incarceration and interrupt the school-to-prison pipeline. However it looks, let us locate ourselves at the juncture of healing and activism, cultivating and practicing a spacious awareness and praxis of both.

Notes

Chapter 1: The Journey to Racial Justice and Restorative Justice

1. The Soledad Brothers were three African American activists and prison inmates, George Jackson, Fleeta Drumgo, and John Clutchette, who faced politically motivated charges of murder of a prison guard in 1970. A defense committee formed to raise funds and campaign for their freedom. After a 1972 trial, they were acquitted of all charges. (Jonathan Jackson, who brandished guns registered to Angela Davis in the takeover of the Marin County courtroom that led to her being placed on the FBI's Ten Most Wanted list, was the younger brother of George Jackson.)
2. Pranis, K. (2006). "Restorative Values." In G. Johnstone and D.W. Van Ness (eds.), *Handbook of Restorative Justice*. Cullompton, Devon, UK: Willan Publishing.

Chapter 2: Ubuntu: The Indigenous Ethos of Restorative Justice

1. Use of the expression *African worldview* or *African-centered view* is not meant to suggest that the continent of Africa is monocultural or homogenous; actually, its diversity of cultural expression appears limitless. Further, Africa's varied cultures were impacted by colonialism's external influences. Even so, certain fundamental principles and values—such as *ubuntu*, egalitarianism, communalism, social equilibrium, extended family, and ancestral reverence—have survived across time and diverse cultures.

2. Elechi, O. (2005). "African Indigenous Justice System." In Richard A. Wright and J. Mitchell Miller (eds.), *Encyclopedia of Criminology* (pp. 18–22). New York: Taylor & Francis.

3. Shutte, A. 1993. *Philosophy for Africa.* Rondebosch, South Africa: UCT Press.

4. Elechi, O. (2005). "African Indigenous Justice System." In Richard A. Wright and J. Mitchell Miller (eds.), *Encyclopedia of Criminology* (pp. 18–22). New York: Taylor & Francis.

5. Zehr, H. (2005). *Changing Lenses: A New Focus for Crime and Justice.* Scottdale, PA: Herald Press, pp. 268–69.

6. Though honoring indigenous roots marks a perceptible shift in the RJ movement, some indigenous people today deny kinship with restorative justice, often expressing concern that restorative justice (narrowly construed as a program or social services) bears no resemblance to authentic indigenous ways.

7. Personal communication, 2004

8. Personal communication, 2018.

9. Axiology refers to values; cosmology to creation stories encoding worldviews; epistemology to ways of knowing; and ontology, ways of being.

10. Colorado, A. (1996). "Indigenous Science: Dr. Pamela Colorado Talks to Jane Carroll." *ReVision* 18(3): 6–10.

11. Thomas Hobbes, considered the founder of modern political philosophy, declared that, where there is no government, no laws, and no common power to restrain human nature, life in the state of nature is "nasty, brutish and short."

12. Elechi, O., S. V. C. Morris, and E. J. Schauer (February 16, 2010). "Restoring Justice (Ubuntu): An African Perspective." *International Criminal Justice Review*, p. 77. Retrieved from: http://journals.sagepub.com/doi/pdf/10.1177/1057567710361719

13. "[T]he incarceration rate of . . . Nigeria, Liberia, Gambia, Mali, and South Africa are 26, 29, 32, 33, and 334, respectively per 100,000 inhabitants. Compare that to other countries such as the United States

of America, 760; Russian Federation, 626; United Kingdom, 152; Canada, 116; and Japan 63, incarceration rate per 100,000 inhabitants." International Centre for Prison Studies at the School of Law, King's College London, 2009.

Chapter 3: Integrating Racial Justice and Restorative Justice

1. Lawrence, K., and T. Keleher (2004). "Structural Racism." The Race and Public Policy Conference, Aspen, Colorado. Retrieved from https://www.intergroup resources.com/rc/Definitions%20of%20Racism.pdf

2. 1,747 hate crimes were reported, a 25.9 percent increase over the same period in 2015, when 1,388 hate crimes were reported. Barrouquere, B. (2017, November 3). "FBI: Hate Crimes Reach 5-year High in 2016, Jumped as Trump Rolled toward Presidency." Southern Poverty Law Center. Retrieved from https://www.splcenter .org/hatewatch/2017/11/13/fbi-hate-crimes-reach -5-year-high-2016-jumped-trump-rolled-toward -presidency-0

3. Hall, A. V., E. V. Hall, and J. L. Perry (2016). Black and Blue: Exploring Racial Bias and Law Enforcement in the Killings of Unarmed Black Male Civilians [Electronic version]. Retrieved from Cornell University, SHA School site: http://scholarship.sha.cornell.edu/articles/887

4. Payne, K., and L. Niemi (March 27, 2018). How to Think about "Implicit Bias." *Scientific American* Retrieved from https://www.scientificamerican.com /article/how-to-think-about-implicit-bias/

5. Smith R., and J. Levinson. (2012). The Impact of Implicit Racial Bias on the Exercise of Prosecutorial Discretion. *Seattle University Law Review,* 35(3).

6. Johnson, T. (December 26, 2014). Black-on-Black Racism: The Hazards of Implicit Bias. *The Atlantic.* Retrieved from https://www.theatlantic.com/politics /archive/2014/12/black-on-black-racism-the-hazards-of -implicit-bias/384028/

7. In the Hindu, Buddhist, and Jain traditions, *ahimsa* is the principle of nonviolence toward all beings.

8. A Sanskrit term coined by Mahatma Gandhi in connection with nonviolent resistance, *satyagraha* is translated as holding firmly onto truth.

9. Chapters 4–6 discuss inequities in detail, such as black people are six times more likely to be incarcerated than whites and nine times more likely to have an incarcerated parent. Black youth are ten times more likely to die of homicide. Latinos and blacks are 30 percent of the population but 60 percent of the nation's prisoners. Hall, A. V., E. V. Hall, and J. L. Perry. (2016). "Black and Blue: Exploring Racial Bias and Law Enforcement in the Killings of Unarmed Black Male Civilians" [Electronic version]. Retrieved from Cornell University, SHA School site: http://scholarship .sha.cornell.edu/articles/887; Kerby, S. (2012, March 13). "The Top 10 Most Startling Facts about People of Color and Criminal Justice in the United States. A Look at the Racial Disparities Inherent in our Nation's Criminal-Justice System." Center for American Progress. Retrieved from https://www.americanprogress.org/issues /race/news/2012/03/13/11351/the-top-10-most-startling -facts-about-people-of-color-and-criminal-justice-in -the-united-states/

10. Black Lives Matter (n.d.). Retrieved from https://black livesmatter.com/about/what-we-believe/

11. Reconstruction refers to the period following the end of the Civil War until 1877, during which the federal government controlled the former Confederate states to facilitate rebuilding the South and to assure the newly emancipated African Americans were conferred full freedom, citizenship, and equality. Unprecedented democratic achievements occurred during this period often referred to as the most democratic era in the nation's history. For instance, blacks were granted the right to vote and voted into power many black elected officials. Also, Reconstruction governments invested in the public infrastructure, extended the vote to landless

whites, established public education in the South for all, and founded charitable institutions to support and care for all citizens.

Chapter 4: Race, Restorative Justice, and Schools

1. Losen, D. J., and T. E. Martinez (2013). "Out of School & Off Track: The Overuse of Suspensions in American Middle and High Schools." The Center for Civil Rights Remedies at The Civil Rights Project/ Proyecto Derechos Civiles, University of California, Los Angeles. Retrieved from https://files.eric.ed.gov /fulltext/ED541731.pdf
2. Ibid.
3. Majerowicz, A. (June 1, 2016). "School Suspensions Cost Taxpayers Billions." The Civil Rights Project/Proyecto Derechos Civiles, University of California, Los Angeles. Retrieved from https://www.civilrightsproject.ucla .edu/news/press-releases/featured-research-2016 /school-suspensions-cost-taxpayers-billions/
4. Resmovits, J. (June 6, 2016). "Black Preschool Kids Get Suspended Much More Frequently than White Preschool Kids, U.S. Survey Says." Los Angeles Times. Retrieved from http://www.latimes.com/local/education /la-na-suspension-rates-preschool-crdc-20160606-snap -story.html
5. Emihovich, C. A. (1983). "The Color of Misbehaving: Two Case Studies of Deviant Boys." Journal of Black Studies, 13(3): 259–74.
6. In the wake of public protest and community organizing, the Los Angeles, San Francisco, and Oakland school districts have banned suspensions for defiance, while the California state legislature banned suspensions for defiance for K–3 students statewide.
7. Morris, M. (2014). "Race, Gender and the School-to-Prison Pipeline: Expanding Our Discussion to Include Black Girls." African American Policy Forum. Retrieved from http://schottfoundation.org/sites/default/files/resources

/Morris-Race-Gender-and-the-School-to-Prison
-Pipeline.pdf

8. *Education Week* (2017). "Policing America's Schools:
An *Education Week* Analysis." Retrieved from https:
//www.edweek.org/ew/projects/2017/policing-americas
-schools/student-arrests.html#/overview

9. Martin, M. (Interviewer), and Stoughton, S. (Interviewee)
(July 9, 2016). "Looking at How Police Are Trained." NPR,
All Things Considered [Interview transcript]. Retrieved
from https://www.npr.org/2016/07/09/485388430/looking
-at-how-police-are-trained

10. "Police in Schools Are Not the Answer to School
Shootings" (2018). Retrieved from http://dignityin
schools.org/wp-content/uploads/2018/03/Police-In
-Schools-2018-FINAL.pdf

11. Gregory, A., D. Cornell, and X. Fan (2011). "The
Relationship of School Structure and Support to
Suspension Rates for Back and White High School
Students." *American Educational Research Journal*.
Retrieved from http://www.indiana.edu/~atlantic
/wp-content/uploads/2011/11/Gregory-et-al.-The
-Relationship-of-School-Structure-and-Support-to
-Suspension-Rates.pdf

12. For a more detailed early history of school-based
restorative justice, see Evans, K., and D. Vaandering
(2016). *The Little Book of Restorative Justice in Education.*
New York: Good Books; and Fronius, T., S. Guckenburg,
N. Hurley, H. Persson, and A. Petrosino (2016)
Restorative Justice in U.S. Schools: A Research Review. San
Francisco, CA: WestEd Justice & Prevention Research
Center.

13. Gonzalez, T. (2012). "Keeping Kids in Schools:
Restorative Justice, Punitive Discipline, and the School
to Prison Pipeline." *Journal of Law and Education*, 41(2):
281–335; see Schiff, M. (2018). "Can Restorative Justice
Disrupt the 'School-to-Prison Pipeline'?" *Contemporary
Justice Review*.

14. Lewis, S. (2009). *Improving School Climate: Findings from
Schools Implementing Restorative Practices.* Bethlehem,

PA: International Institute for Restorative Practices; Mirsky, L. (May 20, 2003). "SaferSanerSchools: Transforming School Culture with Restorative Practices." *Restorative Practices Eforum.* Retrieved from https: //www.iirp.edu/eforum-archive/safersanerschools -transforming-school-culture-with-restorative-practices; and Sumner, D., C. Silverman, and M. Frampton (2010). "School-Based Restorative Justice as an Alternative to Zero-Tolerance Policies: Lessons from West Oakland." Berkeley: University of California, Berkeley, School of Law.

15. Jain, S., H. Bassey, M. Brown, and P. Kalra (2014). "Restorative Justice Implementation and Impacts in Oakland Schools" (prepared for the Office of Civil Rights, US Department of Education). Oakland, CA: Oakland Unified School District, Data in Action.

16. Gonzalez, T. (2012). "Keeping Kids in Schools: Restorative Justice, Punitive Discipline, and the School to Prison Pipeline." *Journal of Law and Education,* 41(2), 281–335.; Jain, S., H. Bassey, M. Brown, and P. Kalra (2014). "Restorative Justice Implementation and Impacts in Oakland Schools" (prepared for the Office of Civil Rights, US Department of Education). Oakland, CA: Oakland Unified School District, Data in Action; and Gregory, A., K. Clawson, A. Davis, and J. Gerewitz (2014). "The Promise of Restorative Practices to Transform Teacher-Student Relationships and Achieve Equity in School Discipline." *Journal of Educational & Psychological Consultation* [Special issue: Restorative Justice].

17. Sumner, D., C. Silverman, and M. Frampton (2010). "School-Based Restorative Justice as an Alternative to Zero-Tolerance Policies: Lessons from West Oakland." Berkeley: University of California, Berkeley, School of Law.

18. Data shared in personal communication with Jean Wing, Executive Director of Research, Assessment and Data, Oakland Unified School District, Sept 7, 2017.

19. Gonzalez, T. (2012). "Keeping Kids in School: Restorative Justice, Punitive Discipline, and the School to Prison Pipeline." *Journal of Law and Education*, 41(2). Retrieved from SSRN: https://ssrn.com/abstract=2658513

20. Gregory, A., D. Cornell, and X. Fan (2011). "The Relationship of School Structure and Support to Suspension Rates for Black and White High School Students." *American Educational Research Journal*. Retrieved from http://www.indiana.edu/~atlantic/wp-content/uploads/2011/11/Gregory-et-al.-The-Relationship-of-School-Structure-and-Support-to-Suspension-Rates.pdf

21. Anyon, Y., and B. Downing (May 2017). "An Exploration of the Relationships between Student Racial Background and the School Sub-contexts of Office Discipline Referrals: A Critical Race Theory Analysis." *Race Ethnicity and Education* 21, no. 3 (2018): 390–406.

Chapter 5: Restorative Justice and Transforming Mass Incarceration

1. Kahan, P. (2008). *Eastern State Penitentiary: A History.* Charleston, SC: The History Press; Eastern State Penitentiary: Timeline (2018). Retrieved from https://www.easternstate.org/research/history-eastern-state/timeline

2. For example, enslaved persons who attempted to escape experienced mutilation, beatings of the naked body until the flesh fell off, and being oiled and set afire while hanging from a tree. Not ending with the abolition of slavery, with lynchings, these macabre practices survived, surging in the late 1800s to reestablish white supremacy after the newly emancipated voted into office black legislators in significant numbers, ushering in Reconstruction, which, though short-lived, was the most democratic era of US governance ever.

3. "Exploiting Black Labor after the Abolition of Slavery" (February 6, 2017). Retrieved from http://theconversation

.com/exploiting-black-labor-after-the-abolition-of
-slavery-72482

4. The chain gang was not actually outlawed until 1955,
and law enforcement authorities brought it back to
Alabama and Arizona in the mid-1990s.

5. Though Jim Crow was legally abolished, anti-lynching
bills have failed to pass the US legislature for two
hundred years.

6. The Sentencing Project (2018). "Fact Sheet: Trends in
U.S. Corrections." Retrieved from https://sentencing
-project.org/wp-content/uploads/2016/01/Trends-in-US
-Corrections.pdf

7. Baum, D. (April 2016). "Legalize It All. How to Win
the War on Drugs." *Harper's*. Retrieved from https:
//harpers.org/archive/2016/04/legalize-it-all

8. Day, E. (February 2, 2018). "The Race Gap in US
Prisons Is Glaring, and Poverty Is Making It Worse."
Mother Jones. Retrieved from https://www.mother
jones.com/crime-justice/2018/02/the-race-gap-in-u-s
-prisons-is-glaring-and-poverty-is-making-it-worse/

9. Hamilton, L. (October 20, 2016). "Liz Ryan Is on a Mission
to Close Youth Prisons." The Annie E. Casey Foundation.
Retrieved from https://www.aecf.org/podcast/liz-ryan-is
-on-a-mission-to-close-youth-prisons/

10. Schanzenback, D., R. Nunn, L. Bauer, A. Breitwieser, M.
Mumford, and G. Nantz (October 2016). "Twelve Facts
about Incarceration and Prisoner Reentry." The Hamilton
Project. Brookings. Retrieved from https://www
.brookings.edu/research/twelve-facts-about-incarceration
-and-prisoner-reentry/

11. Wildra, E. (June 26, 2017). "Incarceration Shortens
Life Expectancy." Prison Policy Initiative. Retrieved
from https://www.prisonpolicy.org/blog/2017/06/26/life
_expectancy/

12. The Pew Charitable Trusts (2010). "Collateral costs:
Incarceration's Effect on Economic Mobility." Retrieved
from https://www.pewtrusts.org/~/media/legacy/uploaded
files/pcs_assets/2010/collateralcosts1pdf.pdf

13. Brown, T., and E. Patterson (June 28, 2016). "Wounds from Incarceration That Never Heal." *The New Republic.* Retrieved from https://newrepublic.com/article/134712 /wounds-incarceration-never-heal

14. "Facts about the Over-incarceration of Women in the United States" (2018). *American Civil Liberties Union.* Retrieved from https://www.aclu.org/other/facts-about -over-incarceration-women-united-states

15. Barnert, E., R. Perry, V. Azzi, R. Shetgiri, G. Ryan, R. Dudovitz, B. Zima, and P. Chung (July 2015). "Incarcerated Youth's Perspectives on Protective Factors and Risk Factors for Juvenile Offending: A Qualitative Analysis." *American Journal of Public Health.* Retrieved from https://www.ncbi.nlm.nih.gov/pmc/articles/PMC44 63382/

16. Johnson, W., and R. Kelley (2018). "Race Capitalism Justice." *Boston Review* Forum 1 Cambridge, MA, 21–22.

17. The share of all income held by the top 1 percent in recent years has approached or surpassed historical highs. "The Unequal States of America: Income Inequality in the United States." Economic Policy Institute website, https://www.epi.org/multimedia/unequal-states -of-america/

18. Lawrence, A. (2013). "Shrinking Prisons: January 2013." *National Conference of State Legislatures Magazine.* Retrieved from http://www.ncsl.org/research/civil-and -criminal-justice/shrinking-prisons.aspx#4

19. Subramanian, R., and R. Delaney (February 2014). "Playbook for Change? States Reconsider Mandatory Sentences." Vera Institute of Justice. Retrieved from https://www.prisonpolicy.org/scans/vera/mandatory -sentences-policy-report-v2b.pdf

20. "91 Percent of Americans Support Criminal Justice Reform" (November 16, 2017). *American Civil Liberties Union.* Retrieved from https://www.aclu .org/news/91-percent-americans-support-criminal -justice-reform-aclu-polling-finds. Since "sending some- one to prison for a long sentence increases the chances that he or she will commit another crime when they

get out because prison doesn't do a good job of reha-
bilitating problems like drug addiction and mental
illness."

21. "130 Top Police Chiefs and Prosecutors Urge End
to Mass Incarceration" (October 21, 2015). Brennan
Center for Justice. Retrieved from https://www.brennan
center.org/press-release/130-top-police-chiefs-and
-prosecutors-urge-end-mass-incarceration

22. Personal communication, November 6, 2018. Kaba,
now located in New York, is working with others in
the Just Outcomes Collaborative to train people across
the country in non-carceral community accountability
processes.

23. Further, research is virtually unanimous in estab-
lishing the greater effectiveness, lower cost, and
increased equity of restorative justice diversion com-
pared to adjudication and incarceration. Latimer, J.,
C. Dowden, and D. Muise (2005). "The Effectiveness
of Restorative Justice Practices: A Meta-analysis." *The
Prison Journal,* 85(2): 127–44; Poulson, B. (2003). "A
Third Voice: A Review of Empirical Research on the
Psychological Outcomes of Restorative Justice." *Utah
Law Review,* 15(9): 167, 196–98; Sherman, L., and H.
Strang (2007). "Restorative Justice: The Evidence." The
Smith Institute. Retrieved from http://www.iirp.edu
/pdf/RJ_full_report.pdf; and O'Mahony, D., and J.
Doak (2017). *Reimagining Restorative Justice: Agency
and Accountability in the Criminal Process.* Portland, OR:
Hart Publishing.

Chapter 6: Toward a Racial Reckoning: Imagining a Truth Process for Police Violence

1. Angelou, M. (1993). "The Inauguration; Maya
Angelou: 'On the Pulse of Morning.'" *New York Times*
Archives. Retrieved from https://www.nytimes.com/1993
/01/21/us/the-inauguration-maya-angelou-on-the
-pulse-of-morning.html

2. TRC calls came from Ford Foundation President
Darren Walker, former NAACP President Ben Jealous,

New York Times columnist Nicholas Kristof, human rights law Professor Ronald C. Slye, Democratic Party official Donna Brazile, civil rights attorney Bryan Stevenson, and others.

3. Two examples are the 1979 Greensboro Klan massacre and the 2017 merciless beating of a black teacher by hate group members in a downtown Charlottesville garage where police were conspicuously absent.

4. The term *reconciliation* is contested and often discredited as acquiescence or reestablishment of a conciliatory state that never was. However, I see it as an ongoing process of establishing and maintaining respectful relationships and, when damaged, restoring them by apology, with individual and collective reparations, and with concrete actions leading to relational and systems change.

5. One officer was found liable in a civil trial for one of the killings.

6. Of note, after the deadly white hate group demonstrations in Charlottesville in 2017, the Greensboro City Council issued an apology for the 1979 Klan-Nazi killings, promising it would also review the GTRC report and recommendations.

7. Llewellyn, J., and D. Philpott, eds. (2014). *Restorative Justice, Reconciliation, and Peacebuilding.* New York: Oxford University Press, pp. 18, 23, 29.

8. Critical race theory is an analytical lens developed in the United States on the heels of the social justice movements of the 1960s and 1970s by public intellectuals to examine power structures.

9. Community ownership of a truth and reconciliation process in response to mass harm has precedent in Sierra Leone, West Africa, where the ancient practice of Fambul Tok (or "family talk") has been revived to address issues arising from a brutal civil war. This process brings together multiple voices—religious and political leaders, influential community members, youth, war victims, former combatants—for a "family talk" and traditional truth-telling and forgiveness ceremonies. Fambul Tok emphasizes reconciliation, viewed

as the restoration of dignity and strong communities, as an ongoing community healing process that continues after the "family talk" is over. Fambul Tok is succeeding where Western-oriented international peacebuilding efforts have failed.

10. Blinder, A., and R. Fausset (January 26, 2017). "Nearly 8 Decades Later, an Apology for a Lynching in Georgia." *New York Times*.

11. David M. Kennedy is professor of criminal justice at John Jay College of Criminal Justice in New York City and director of the National Network for Safe Communities at John Jay. Mr. Kennedy and the National Network support several jurisdictions and police executives across the nation in implementing strategic interventions to reduce violence, minimize arrest and incarceration, enhance police legitimacy, and strengthen relationships between law enforcement and communities.

12. Residency requirements ensure that police officers are residents of the community they are serving, promoting greater relationality and accountability and reducing the likelihood that officers will use lethal violence.

Chapter 7: A Way Forward

1. It bears mentioning that even though the idea of reparations is today gaining an unprecedented level of mainstream acceptance, the movement for reparations has been underway continuously in the United States dating back to slavery. The National Coalition for Blacks for Reparations in America has been carrying the banner in the contemporary era since the 1960s.

2. A few examples include: DiAngelo, R. (2018). *White Fragility: Why It's So Hard for White People to Talk About Racism.* Boston, MA: Beacon Press; DiAngelo, R. (2016). *What Does It Mean to Be White?: Developing White Racial Literacy.* New York: Counterpoints; Irving,

D. (2014). *Waking Up White and Finding Myself in the Story of Race*. Cambridge, MA: Elephant Rooms Press; and Painter, N. I. (2011). *The History of White People*. New York: Norton.

Acknowledgments

The generous support of Restorative Justice for Oakland Youth and the Annie E. Casey Foundation facilitated completion of this book, and for it, I am exceedingly grateful. The dedicated and skilled assistance of my editor Barb Toews was also crucial. Acknowledgment is further due to all my restorative justice colleagues who made important contributions through our conversations, particularly to the chapters on schools and the justice system, including Lauren Abramson, Yoli Anyon, Teiahsha Bankhead, Ellen Barry, Tyrone Botelho, sujatha baliga, Thalia Gonzales, Sonia Jain, Mariame Kaba, Katy Miller, Kay Pranis, Nancy Reistenberger, Danielle Sered, and David Yusem. I offer gratitude to my sister Angela Davis who helped me conceptualize the book and to my daughter Angela Eisa Davis for her loving support throughout the process, especially her editorial assistance and her help with the chapter on envisioning a truth process for the United States. Margaret Burnham's, Jennifer Llewelyn's, and Brenda Morrison's ideas and work also influenced the truth process chapter. Finally, for their inimitable wisdom and love, I offer a deep bow of gratitude to my extraordinary indigenous elders Vusamazulu Credo Mutwa and Gonondo Sheila Mbele Khama.

About the Author

Fania E. Davis is a leading national voice on the intersection of racial and restorative justice. She is a long-time social justice activist, civil rights trial attorney, restorative justice practitioner, and writer and scholar with a PhD in indigenous knowledge. Coming of age in Birmingham, Alabama, during the social ferment of the civil rights era, the murder of two close childhood friends in the 1963 Sunday school bombing crystallized within Fania a passionate commitment to social transformation. For the next decades, she was active in the civil rights, black liberation, women's, prisoners', peace, anti-racial violence, and anti-apartheid movements. Study with indigenous healers, particularly in Africa, catalyzed her search for a healing justice, ultimately leading Fania to bring restorative justice to Oakland, California. Founding director of Restorative Justice of Oakland Youth (RJOY), her numerous honors include the Ubuntu Award for Service to Humanity, the Dennis Maloney Award for Youth-Based Community and Restorative Justice, the Tikkun Olam (Repair the World) Award, the Ella Jo Baker Human Rights Award, the Bioneers Change Maker Award, and the EBONY Power 100 Community Crusaders Award. She is a Woodrow Wilson fellow, and the *Los Angeles Times* named her a "New Civil Rights Leader of the 21st Century."

Group Discounts for

The Little Book of
Race and Restorative Justice
ORDER FORM

If you would like to order multiple copies of *The Little Book of Race and Restorative Justice* for groups you know or are a part of, please email **bookorders@skyhorsepublishing.com** or fax order to **(212) 643-6819**. (Discounts apply only for more than one copy.)

Photocopy this page and the next as often as you like.

The following discounts apply:

1 copy	$5.99
2-5 copies	$5.39 each (a 10% discount)
6-10 copies	$5.09 each (a 15% discount)
11-20 copies	$4.79 each (a 20% discount)
21-99 copies	$4.19 each (a 30% discount)
100 or more	$3.59 each (a 40% discount)

Free Shipping for orders of 100 or more!

Prices subject to change.

Quantity	The Little Book of Race and	Price	Total
_____ copies of	Restorative Justice @	_____	_____

(Standard ground shipping costs will be added for orders of less than 100 copies.)

METHOD OF PAYMENT

❒   Check or Money Order
      *(payable to **Skyhorse Publishing** in U.S. funds)*

❒   Please charge my:
❒ MasterCard ❒ Visa
❒ Discover   ❒ American Express
_____

Exp. date and sec. code_____

Signature _____

Name _____

Address _____

City_____

State _____

Zip_____

Phone_____

Email _____

SHIP TO: (if different)
Name _____

Address _____

City_____

State _____

Zip_____

Call: (212) 643-6816
Fax: (212) 643-6819
Email: bookorders@skyhorsepublishing.com
(do not email credit card info)